"Finally, a book which rightly puts the struggle with purity, pornography and sexuality into the larger biblical framework of what it means to know God in the midst of our brokenness! This is a wonderful resource to add to the arsenal of anyone serious about finding freedom from the power of pornography. In addition to that, Tim has written a book that can be effectively used by pastors and leaders. It is an excellent pastoral tool to help those dealing with and impacted by the false promises and lies of our porn-is-the-norm culture."

JOHN FREEMAN, *president, Harvest USA (www.harvestusa.org)*

"Tim Chester has hit the nail on the head! Pornography is a cancer eating the heart of the church, and this excellent book tackles it head-on. As you would expect, it is thoroughly rooted in the Bible, very well researched and highly accessible. Crucially, Tim also offers fantastic practical and realistic help and advice that us men would do well to take advantage of. I highly commend this timely book."

CARL BEECH, *general director, Christian Vision for Men (www.men.org.uk)*

"Tim Chester believes that churches need to talk about porn, and has written a helpful book that explains why. I believe it will be a lifeline for those who feel trapped and say, 'I can't change.' It contains a message of grace, strength and hope."

IAN COFFEY, *director of leadership training, Moorlands College*

"Christians think sex is great, but its misuse is bad! Pornography draws Christian men into a dark world where shame and guilt replace joy and freedom. This book superbly diagnoses the problem and points to God's healing. Tim Chester's writing will rescue many a marriage and restore many a man to a place where purity and passion coexist in biblical relationship."

STEPHEN AND JANET GAUKROGER, *Clarion Trust International*

"Tim Chester offers hope, and the possibility of living free from the snare of pornography. . . . Without sounding superspiritual or piling on the guilt, this book emphasizes the fact that we cannot change without God's help. . . . Chester's diligent research and nonjudgmental approach will, I promise, help many Christians who are struggling with porn."

Lyndon Bowring, *executive chairman, CARE*

"One of the greatest challenges facing Christians today is the call to sexual purity and integrity. Tim Chester's book will prove indispensable for those committed to that challenge. By exposing the lies that fuel pornography addiction and offering practical tips for staying free, he arms us with the tools we need to win the battle against porn."

Andy Comiskey, *founder and director, Desert Stream Ministries, and author of* Naked Surrender: Coming Home to Our True Sexuality

Closing the Window

Steps to Living Porn Free

TIM CHESTER

IVP Books

An imprint of InterVarsity Press
Downers Grove, Illinois

InterVarsity Press
P.O. Box 1400, Downers Grove, IL 60515-1426
World Wide Web: www.ivpress.com
E-mail: email@ivpress.com

InterVarsity Press® is the book-publishing division of InterVarsity Christian Fellowship/USA®, a movement of students and faculty active on campus at hundreds of universities, colleges and schools of nursing in the United States of America, and a member movement of the International Fellowship of Evangelical Students. For information about local and regional activities, write Public Relations Dept., InterVarsity Christian Fellowship/USA, 6400 Schroeder Rd., P.O. Box 7895, Madison, WI 53707-7895, or visit the IVCF website at <www.intervarsity.org>.

All Scripture quotations, unless otherwise indicated, are taken from the Holy Bible, New International Version®. NIV®. *Copyright ©1973, 1978, 1984 by International Bible Society. Used by permission of Zondervan Publishing House. All rights reserved.*

Design: Cindy Kiple
Images: Roel Smart/iStockphoto

ISBN 978-0-8308-3842-4

Printed in the United States of America ∞

Library of Congress Cataloging-in-Publication Data

Chester, Tim.
   Closing the window: steps to living porn free / Tim Chester.
      p. cm.
   Includes bibliographical references (p.   ).
   ISBN 978-0-8308-3842-4 (pbk.: alk. paper)
   1. Pornography—Religious aspects—Christianity. I. Title.
BV4597.6.C44 2010
241'.667—dc22

                                                                              2010019859

P	18	17	16	15	14	13	12	11	10	9	8	7	6	5	4	3	2	1
Y	25	24	23	22	21	20	19	18	17	16	15	14	13	12	11	10		

Contents

Introduction

Let's Talk About Porn

TODAY THERE IS AN EPIDEMIC of pornography.

There are two factors behind this growth. The first is an increasingly permissive attitude in our society. What would have been considered porn a generation ago has become part of mainstream culture.

Women in various states of undress, or indicating sexual availability, commonly appear in music videos, television programs, movies and advertisements. Young women wear T-shirts emblazoned with the words "Porn Star" or "Sex Kitten." The number of sex scenes on U.S. television nearly doubled between 1998 and 2005.[1] You can buy pole-dancing equipment for your home from mainstream online retailers. Softcore porn has moved off the top shelf into "young men's mags." Meanwhile, hardcore porn "has evolved and is increasingly dominated by the sadomasochistic themes of forced sex, ejaculations on women's faces, and angry anal sex, all involving scripts fusing sex with hatred and humiliation."[2]

Pamela Paul talks about a "pornified" culture: "Not only is pornography itself more ubiquitous, the entire culture has become pornified. By that, I mean that the aesthetics, values, and standards of pornography have seeped into mainstream popular culture."[3]

Jonny describes it like this: "Imagine being an alcoholic and everywhere you go they use free beer to sell things. I'm free from porn at the moment, but it's a constant battle. I feel like I'm constantly being offered this drug that I know can destroy my life."

There was a time when sexual addiction was strongly correlated to childhood abuse or trauma. But the saturation of our culture with sex and pornography means this is no longer the case. Many people from good families are nevertheless mired in porn.

The second factor behind the acceleration of porn comes in the form of new technologies that can deliver porn into the home. A few centuries ago the wealthy few bought salacious books and illustrations. Then magazines turned porn into a mass-market industry. Videos and DVDs took it to another level. But, more than anything else, the Internet has accelerated its spread. The Internet not only brought a virtually unlimited supply of porn directly into the home, but also took away the point of shame. Previously, you had to buy a porn magazine from a real person across the counter and risk being seen by someone you knew; now, porn can be consumed in secret. Again and again, people talk about the Internet accelerating their involvement in porn. The following statements are typical:

> It was at university that things got much worse. I had my own room with a fast Internet connection so there was nothing to hold me back.

> At seventeen I became a Christian and the addiction began to weaken. For a few years it had virtually no hold over me. However, with access to the Internet it became a problem again. Since then I was accessing porn on an almost daily basis.

> When Internet came [to the theological college where I was], it was like the child in a candy store with no parents around.

Psychologist Dr. Alvin Cooper talks about "the triple-A engine" that drives cybersex and make it so enticing:

- accessibility
- anonymity
- affordability[4]

ONE IN THREE

Not only is our culture becoming "pornified," so too is the church. A recent survey found that 50 percent of Christian men and 20 percent of Christian women are "addicted to porn."[5] That means that in a church with one hundred adults, twenty-five men and ten women are struggling with porn: one in three. I'm suspicious of sex surveys because people so often lie about sex—either exaggerating their sexual activity or hiding their sexual secrets. This survey of one thousand people was conducted online, which might suggest that these figures are higher than the norm, since Internet users are obviously more likely to view porn. On the other hand, Christians are likely to understate their problem, to view it as a past problem or a temporary issue. The shame factor suggests that the figures may be understated. So perhaps, overall, taken on balance, the survey results are close to reality. *Christianity Today* reported one evangelical leader who was skeptical of the survey findings, so he surveyed the men in his congregation. He found that 60 percent had looked at porn within the past year and 25 percent within the past thirty days.[6]

Think about your own church or house group. It's possible that *one in three* people is struggling with porn. And if you find that unlikely, then the chances are that most of these people are struggling alone, feeling unable to talk about it.

Another survey reported that 33 percent of church leaders and 36 percent of church members had visited a sexually explicit site in the past year.[7] An Internet survey conducted by Rick Warren of Saddleback Church in Southern California found that 30 percent of six thousand pastors had viewed Internet porn in the last thirty days.[8] The same proportions again: one in three.

Among young Christians the proportion is still higher. A student worker ministering with young Christian men in a British university emailed me, saying, "I have only come across *one* person who does not struggle with porn and addictive masturbation. . . . I also spend time mentoring single young men in [a well-known mission agency] and I would say the porn addiction rate is about 60-70 percent." Another minister reported to me that *every* man under forty in his congregation has struggled with porn. A student in "a large and well-reputed Bible College" reports that a counselor to whom he went to talk about his struggle with pornography told him "he was seeing a vast number of both married and single men from the college about the same issue."

LET'S TALK ABOUT PORN

We need to start talking about porn in the church. Martin Luther is reported to have said, "If you preach the gospel in all aspects with the exception of the issues that deal specifically with your time, you are not preaching the gospel at all."[9] Al Mohler describes what he calls "the pervasive plague of pornography" as "one of the greatest moral challenges faced by the Christian church in the postmodern age."[10]

In our churches we need to talk about porn. Don't assume people are free from porn until they tell you they're not. Ask the question. Ask everyone you disciple or pastor whether porn is an issue for them.

I suggest we need to teach on sex in our churches at least once a year and to apply other sermons to sexual issues. And we need to do so without being too coy. It's not enough to talk about "maintaining sexual purity"—many people don't know what this involves. Jesus and John the Baptist made repentance specific for people (Luke 3:10-14; 18:22). We have a generation of young people for whom the call to repentance must include a call to turn from porn.

This means proclaiming life without porn as good news. Porn is providing the sex education for a generation of young people, setting their expectations for sex and marriage. This represents a huge challenge for our society. But I also believe it is an opportunity for the church. For years our culture has found the biblical view of sex prudish and old-fashioned. But a time may come when a strong positive message about the joy of sex as an expression of covenantal fidelity may be what people long to hear.[11]

This book is an attempt to start that conversation. It aims to give hope both to those struggling with porn and to those helping others who struggle. I'm generally addressing it to those who are struggling, to avoid repeating myself. But those helping others should readily be able to adapt what I say to those whom they are helping.

What is porn? And when does porn become art? These questions are not always easy to define when framing public policy. But that is not the concern of this book. I'm interested in people who use porn but who want to be free of it. *Porn*, for our purposes, is anything we use for sexual titillation, gratification or escape—whether it was intended for that purpose or not. Much of the time this will be sexually explicit material in magazines or movies, and on the Internet. But it can also involve looking at ads or catalogs to stimulate your lust, or "undressing" people with your eyes, or fantasizing about sex with someone who's not your spouse. We will not concern ourselves with the intention of the person who created the image or narrative or look. We're concerned with the purpose to which you put that image. We'll take as our starting point the words of Jesus: "You have heard that it was said, 'Do not commit adultery.' But I tell you that anyone who looks at a woman lustfully has already committed adultery with her in his heart" (Matthew 5:27-28).

Most of my examples are of men. I don't tend to talk to women about their sexuality, except together with their husbands in the context of marriage. But women also struggle: 28 percent of people visiting pornography sites are women. As we've noted, one survey found that 20 percent of Christian women struggle. Women's use of porn is generally different from that of men—less visually oriented, with a preference for erotic fiction or erotic sections in romantic novels. Women are also twice as likely as men to favor chatrooms.[12] Sue writes:

I would really like it to be acknowledged that this can be a problem for women as well as men. For me, pornographic images are not particularly erotic, but erotic fiction is extremely powerful. Female masturbation is a genuine issue too—perhaps especially for single women—and again, something that I've never heard acknowledged. These issues are always assumed to be gender specific and, as such, it makes it even harder for women to admit when they're struggling in these areas.

It can be especially hard for women to talk about an issue that is often seen as a "male weakness." Jackie says, "I've never told another Christian. I think we're told so often that this isn't a problem for women and this makes it even harder to admit that actually it is a problem for me." In the church we all too often put women in one of two categories. We have the chaste vision of beauty, refinement and godliness epitomized by the Virgin Mary. On the other hand, we have the seductress leading men astray, epitomized by the harlot. We don't have much in between. But "in between" is where real women actually live.

In researching this book I conducted an anonymous online survey through my blog, www.timchester.co.uk. Thank you to everyone who took part. There were 108 responses, half from the United Kingdom, a quarter from the United States, a tenth from Australia and the rest from thirteen other countries in six continents. Of these, 93 percent were men and 7 percent were women. Just under half were in their twenties, a third were in their thirties. The survey was aimed at Christians, so 99 percent currently attended a church and 57 percent were in some position of church leadership. Two-thirds were married and a third were single, with three widowed or divorced respondents. The vast majority thought using porn was sinful. Of all respondents, 30 percent no longer used pornography, 50 percent continued to struggle and 20 percent didn't specify.

Most of the questions asked for open-ended text responses. I've woven many of those responses throughout the book. I've often attributed names to the quotes I've used, but none of those names is real.

A WARNING AND A REASSURANCE

Reading about porn is dangerous. Describing sexual activity provokes thoughts of sexual activity, which create temptations. I'm grateful to those who have prayed for me as I've written this book. And I pray that readers too will be kept from temptation as they read. Not without reason Paul says: "Have nothing to do with the fruitless deeds of darkness, but rather expose them. For it is shameful even to mention what the disobedient do in secret" (Ephesians 5:11-12). I will be frank in this book. There's no point writing a book on pornography that's so coy that its central challenge is missed. But I will avoid unnecessarily describing "what the disobedient do in secret," even as I "expose" "the fruitless deeds of darkness." I suggest that, whenever you put the book down, spend a few moments in prayer and praise. Make sure when you finish reading that you're thinking about Christ and not about porn.

I want you to read this book without fear. If you struggle with porn, then your heart will be exposed. And what you see will be ugly—very ugly—unbearably ugly, but for the grace of God. This book will probably condemn you, but it ought not to leave you condemned, for "there is now no condemnation for those who are in Christ Jesus" (Romans 8:1). The central chapter is on God's grace for porn users. Whatever we discover about our sin, we will discover that God's grace is sufficient.

At the cross we see the horrible extent of our sin. When we get the chance, we kill our Creator. Martin Luther says:

> You must be overwhelmed by the frightful wrath of God who so hated sin that he spared not his only begotten Son. . . . Take this to heart and doubt not that you are the one who killed Christ. Your sins certainly did, and when you see the nails driven through his hands, be sure that you are pounding, and when the thorns pierce his brow, know that they are your evil thoughts.[13]

Yet at the very same time we see in the cross the amazing love of God toward sinners. The sight that exposes our sin is the exact same sight that reveals God's grace. The moment of despair is the moment of hope. Jesus cried from the cross, "It is finished!" It *is* finished. There is nothing left to do; nothing left to pay. The guilt of your porn habit is canceled if your faith is in Christ and his cross. Our sin is great, but God's grace is always greater. "Where sin increased, grace increased all the more, so that, just as sin reigned in death, so also grace might reign through righteousness to bring eternal life through Jesus Christ our Lord" (Romans 5:20-21).

1

Looking Beyond the Frame

HE TOLD ME HE'D USED PORN AGAIN. We talked about his problem. We prayed together. Then I said, "The first thing we need to do is to put accountability software on your computer." His face dropped. He was devastated. I could see it as clear as day. He didn't want to be a porn user, but he still wanted to use porn. Perhaps he would try to change, but he still wanted the option of going to porn.

Christians usually feel a sense of shame about their use of porn. They know it's wrong. They tell you that they want to stop. Except, of course, that they don't stop. They still enjoy porn. Andrew Comiskey of Desert Stream Ministries says that many men he's counseled have recognized their sin, but "the deep recesses of their hearts still contained the will and desire to sin; at some basic level, they remained open and even playful to union with evil."[1]

The reality is that often we dislike the shame and the consequences of sin, but we still like the sin itself. We dislike the shame of porn, but in reality we still want to view it. That's because porn is pleasurable. Let's be honest about that. If we pretend otherwise, we'll never fight it successfully. People like watching porn—otherwise they wouldn't watch. The Bible talks about the pleasures of sin. They're temporary. They're dangerous. They're empty pleasures, compared with the glory of God. But they are pleasures, nonetheless.

Added to this, we have a hundred and one ways to rationalize sin; to explain why it's not so bad; to make it sound inevitable. We say things like:

- It's OK, because it releases my sexual tension.
- It's OK, because everyone involved is enjoying themselves.
- It's OK, because it'll make me a better lover.
- It's OK, because my wife is tired.
- It's OK, because I'm single.

FIVE KEY INGREDIENTS

I'd like to suggest five key ingredients that need to be in place if you're going to win your battle with porn. Here's the first: *an abhorrence of porn—a hatred of porn itself (not just the shame it brings) and a longing for change.* "I can't say that any strategy in particular has helped," says Geoff, "because actually for me it was a matter of wanting to change." Steve Gallagher, founding president of Pure Life Ministries, says,

> A man will never have a pure heart as long as he equivocates about the sinfulness of lust. . . . If he is indecisive on this point, he will never have the courage to win the battle that lies before him. His constant waffling will weaken any resolve to do the hard thing.[2]

Or you may be someone who has never used porn. Perhaps you're reading this book because you want to help someone else. Talking about porn is intriguing. Your curiosity is stirred. You're in a dangerous place. Listen to Paul's warning: "Dear brothers and sisters, if another believer is overcome by some sin, you who are godly should gently and humbly help that person back onto the right path. And be careful not to fall into the same temptation yourself" (Galatians 6:1 NLT). So let me give you twelve good reasons not to get curious; not to touch porn at all.

Table 1. First Key Ingredient in the Battle Against Porn

1	abhorence of porn	a hatred of porn itself (not just the shame it brings) and a longing for change
2	adoration of God	a desire for God, arising from a confidence that he offers more than porn
3	assurance of grace	an assurance that you are loved by God and right with God through faith in the work of Jesus
4	avoidance of temptation	a commitment to do all in your power to avoid temptation, starting with controls on your computer
5	accountability to others	a community of Christians who are holding you accountable and supporting you in your struggle

TWELVE REASONS TO GIVE UP PORN

The following reasons are not all of equal weight, although all of them provide sufficient reason in their own right not to view porn. If we're going to fight porn, we must scratch at its shiny surface to see its ugly heart.

1. PORN WRECKS YOUR VIEW OF SEX

The sex in porn is not real sex. It's not how real people make love. What appears to be one continuous piece of action has actually been filmed in small chunks. The "stud" who just keeps on going has actually been taking breaks throughout. Plus, these days, he's helped along by Viagra, the use of which is now widespread in the porn industry. In real life the sex in porn movies would be impractical. Porn actress Harmony tells Craig Gross, founder of XXX church.com, "It's not how it seems on the videos. It's work, and we have to be in very awkward positions for guys to see the action. It's not real sex. It's actually like mechanical sex."[3] Even supposedly amateur porn is not real sex, because the introduction of a camera radically changes the nature of intercourse, morphing it into a performance.

So watching porn radically distorts our expectations of sex. "Porn wrecked me," says Sean. "It's not as though I recall a particular porn movie that I watched, but the general debasing of sex as God intended is burned in my mind." Leon's experience is similar: "I now have a tainted view of sex which doesn't match the view of the Bible. Sex becomes a seedy thing rather than a good gift from a gracious God."

Sex therapist Aline Zoldbrod believes that many young men today are terrible lovers. "In real life, sexually speaking, women are crock pots [or slow cookers] and men are microwaves. But in pornography all a man does is touch a woman and she's howling in delight. Today, pornography is so widely used by young men, they learn these falsehoods. There's good evidence that the more porn men watch, the less satisfied they are with their partner's looks and sexual performance."[4] Porn has a double effect: dulling people's appetite for real sex while ratcheting up their appetite for more extreme fantasy sex. "At times it caused me to view my wife inappropriately," says Jamal, "and to consider doing acts with her that I knew were inappropriate."

It's not only that we have a distorted view of what happens during sexual intercourse. Our view of sex becomes detached from relationship and intimacy. Sex in porn is just a physical activity, nothing more. But real sex, sex as God intended, is the celebration and climax—quite literally—of a relationship. Godly sex is part of a package that includes talking together, sharing together, deciding together, crying together, working together, laughing together and forgiving each other. Orgasm comes at the end of a process that began with offering a compliment, doing the chores, recalling your day, unburdening your heart, tidying the house. Sex that disregards these things is hollow. It will drive you apart, rather than bring you together as God intended. If you view sex as personal gratification or a chance to enact your fantasy, if you have sex while disregarding intimacy or unresolved conflict, then that sex will be bad in both senses of the word: poor quality and ungodly.

So we see that many men are getting their sex education from porn. This is where they are learning—or think they are learning—what women want and how to "perform" "good" sex. But it's a rubbish education! Porn will teach you *nothing* about good sex. Porn only teaches you to be a porn addict. "Countless men have described to me how," reports Pamela Paul, "while using porn, they have lost the ability to relate or be close to women. They have trouble being turned on by 'real' women, and their sex lives with their girlfriends or wives collapse."[5] A study of college students found that frequent exposure to pornography was associated with the following attitudes:

- increased tolerance toward sexually explicit material, thereby requiring more novel or bizarre material to achieve the same level of arousal or interest

- misperceptions about exaggerated sexual activity in the general populace and the prevalence of less common sexual practices

- acceptance of promiscuity as a normal state of interaction

- viewing sexual inactivity or abstinence as a health risk

- diminished trust in intimate partners

- decreased desire to achieve sexual exclusivity with a partner

- cynicism about love

- believing superior sexual satisfaction is attainable without affection for one's partner

- believing marriage is sexually confining

- finding childrearing an unattractive prospect[6]

Do you want to think like this?

2. PORN WRECKS YOUR VIEW OF WOMEN

My weekend newspaper always has a restaurant review. I only read it if the restaurant scores just one or two out of ten. I'm afraid it's the bad reviews I find interesting! We've grown used to scoring and ranking products. Reviews award movies a number of stars. Websites enable consumers to score products.

Have you ever scored the physical features of a woman? Perhaps with your friends you've given a woman an eight out of ten for her breasts, or ranked the women at work according to their appearance.

Porn encourages men to view women as objects to be consumed. We are "king consumer," clicking through the webpages until we find the "product" that meets our specification. Jack says, "Porn changed the way I perceived women. Instead of complete people, I would see them as lust objects there to satisfy me. My struggle is now to see women as Christ does and not through my sin." Pamela Paul says, "Because pornography involves looking at women but not interacting with them, it elevates the physical while ignoring or trivializing all other aspects of the woman. A woman is literally reduced to her body parts and sexual behaviour."[7] This attitude then spills over into the rest of our lives. Men's magazines grade women by getting their readers to vote for the sexiest looking. Normal relationships become "pornified." A study by the American Psychological Association concluded:

> The sexualization of girls is not just shattering the lives of girls and women, it is preventing boys and young men from relating to girls and women as complex human beings with so much to offer them. It is preventing boys from forming healthy friendships and working relationships with girls and women.[8]

Colin says, "I've found it hard to form good relationships with attractive young women as I've found it hard to disassociate them from the images I've viewed." And Dwayne adds, "I'm single, and porn is probably one of the reasons why—it distorted my view of women."

And it gets worse. A recent analysis of the fifty bestselling adult videos revealed "a grim 'reality' characterized by inequality and violence." Nearly half of the 304 scenes analyzed contained verbal aggression, while over 88 percent showed physical aggression.[9] Robert Jensen concludes: "We live in a rape culture. . . . Women are objectified and women's sexuality is commodified. Sex is sexy because men are dominant and women are subordinate; power is eroticized."[10] A number of studies have found that people exposed to pornographic material were significantly less sympathetic toward victims of rape.[11]

Studies show that most people think that other people's behavior is influenced by pornography, but only a minority acknowledge that their own behavior is so influenced.[12] Wake up! Don't be self-deluded. Porn corrodes your thinking.

3. PORN WRECKS WOMEN'S VIEW OF THEMSELVES

Porn not only wrecks the way you view women; it also wrecks the way women view themselves. The pressure on women to have bodies that match those of the movie and porn actresses is immense. A Western woman has many freedoms and rights. But she also lives in a culture that is "more sexually coarse, explicit, confusing and risky than that of past eras."[13] She has to navigate sexual expectations, impossible standards of attractiveness and aggressive sexual activity. Naomi Wolf says women can't compete, and they know it.

> How can a real woman—with pores and her own breasts and even sexual needs of her own . . . possibly compete with a cyber-vision of perfection, downloadable and extinguishable at will, who comes, so to speak, utterly submissive and tailored to the consumer's least specification? . . . Today, real naked women are just bad porn.[14]

A report of the American Psychological Association concludes:

> The saturation of sexualized images of females is leading to body hatred, eating disorders, low self-esteem, depression, high rates of teen pregnancy and unhealthy sexual development in our girl children. It also leads to impaired cognitive performance. In short, if we tell girls that looking "hot" is the only way to be validated, rather than encouraging them to be active players in the world, they under-perform at everything else.[15]

4. THE PORN INDUSTRY ABUSES WOMEN

The image that porn likes to portray is that of people enjoying themselves. An industry bent on making money tries to add a veneer of respectability by saying it stands for sexual pleasure and freedom. But it is a veneer. The reality is that participants in porn movies are frequently on drugs to dull the pain. It is common for women to vomit between shoots.

> Alcohol, cocaine, heroin, crack and crystal meth blaze through porn workers' bodies, burning through nearly every dollar they make. . . . The purpose of high-powered drugs for most porn performers is to numb themselves, enabling them to blurrily fast-forward through the punishment they're putting their bodies through so that their minds can't catch up with the consequences until much later, assuming they live that long.[16]

Shelley Lubben is a former porn actress now committed to helping women in the industry. Her organization, The Pink Cross Foundation, has compiled a video. It's a sequence of still photographs of porn actresses and actors. Over each picture come words of explanation:

> Haley Paige, died from possible murder and drugs in 2007. . . . Savannah died from self-inflicted gunshot wound in 1994. . . . Kristi Lynn drove at 100 mph and died in a car accident in 1995. . . . Chloë Jones died from liver failure due to alcohol and drugs in 2005. . . . Anastasia Blue died from suicide overdose of Tylenol, July 19, 2008. . . . Eva Lux died from heroin overdose in 2005. . . . Taylor Summers was murdered during a bondage scene."

On and on it goes, for over seven minutes. Eighty-two porn stars in all: just some of the hundreds who've died in tragic circumstances.

It's very common for women involved in porn to have experienced sexual abuse as children or to have had abusive or distant or absent fathers.[17] They're desperate for male approval, and this desperation is exploited by the porn industry. Ex–porn star Amber told Craig Gross how girls are coerced and set up for a shoot. When they show up, there are six guys instead of one. The producers harass the girls if they refuse to continue. "And these young girls," explained Amber, "are going to do it because they're so insecure about themselves and they let these people take advantage of them."[18]

Each year, an estimated two to four million people are trafficked within countries. Women make up 80 percent of people trafficked, and 70 percent of these women are used for sexual purposes. Most of them find themselves forced into prostitution. In United Kingdom brothels, 85 percent of prostitutes are from overseas.[19] And there is a link between trafficking and pornography.[20] A survey of 854 prostitutes in nine countries found that half of them had had pornographic films made of them while in prostitution. Martin Saunders comments: "Consider then the hypocrisy of the activist Christian who vows to help 'Stop the Traffik,' then returns to his PC in secret to help fuel it. By viewing pornography, we're not only engaging in lust; we could also be participating in human rights abuses."[21]

5. PORN IS A SIN AGAINST YOUR WIFE

Jesus is quite clear. "You have heard that it was said, 'Do not commit adultery.' But I tell you that anyone who looks at a woman lustfully has already committed adultery with her in his heart" (Matthew 5:27-28). Every time you look at porn, you're committing adultery with the women you look at. It means you may have already committed adultery against your wife a hundred times, a thousand times.

How will your wife feel when she finds out? Perhaps you already know. The wife of a porn user wrote, "I feel violated—the trust of our marriage is violated over and over again." Bob acknowledges, "Porn has damaged my marriage, to be honest. It means I don't delight in my wife as much, because I've looked at other women. It's also hurt my wife, because I've essentially cheated on her by masturbating over other women." Dave says, "Porn has put more strain on our relationship than anything else, by a long shot. My wife finds it terribly difficult to understand and deal with. She says it makes her feel unloved and affects her body image. After seeing some porn I'd looked at, she said, 'I'm just not like those girls.' "

Studies of women married to porn users have found it has a devastating impact: "effects such as fatigue, changes in appetite and libido, and other signs and symptoms of anxiety and depression, including suicidality."[22] Some researchers liken the consequences to the symptoms of post-traumatic stress disorder.

Themes included seeing oneself as the reason for a partner's excessive pornography use ("I am not attractive enough," "I should be more available"); seeing the partner as uncaring or selfish ("If he loved me, he wouldn't hurt me this way," "I've told him it bothers me and he still uses pornography; he must not care about me"); and viewing the relationship as a farce ("We pretend like everything is fine, but really our relationship is sick and unhealthy").[23]

Is this what you want your wife to be thinking?

Not only have you committed adultery against your wife, but, as we've seen, there is every chance that porn has corrupted your relationship with her and your sex life. The secret that you hide from your wife will create a barrier in your relationship. You may criticize her in order to feel better about your own shortcomings. You will distance yourself from her to avoid any chance of exposure. Jonas says, "Because of the guilt and inherent dishonesty, I felt very alienated from my wife, making me very cold towards her and becoming cruel and aloof." In some cases you may even pick a fight or find fault with your wife, to justify your porn use.

You will start to view sex with your wife not as the celebration of your love, but as reenacted porn. What matters is no longer the relationship but the performance. This means you may be committing adultery against your wife even as you have sex with her. That's because you're not really having sex with her, as a person. You've reduced her to an object for your sexual gratification, or an actress in your sexual performance.

If you're not yet married, *porn is a sin against your future wife*. You're already committing adultery against a wife with whom you're not even yet married. You're also creating a set of expectations that bears no relation to real sex or real marriage. You're storing up a database of images that will compete with your future wife. You're gifting the devil with a reservoir of temptation to use against you. "The pictures stay in your head for years," Craig warns; "I can still picture some of them now." Al Mohler says, "The deliberate use of pornography is nothing less than the willful invitation of illicit lovers and objectified sex objects and forbidden knowledge into a man's heart, mind, and soul."[24] You're to steward your body so that you can truly use it to love and serve your future wife. Naomi Wolf puts it like this:

> An orgasm is one of the biggest reinforcers imaginable. If you associate orgasm with your wife, a kiss, a scent, a body, that is what, over time, will turn you on; if you open your focus to an endless stream of ever-more-transgressive images of cybersex slaves, that is what it will take to turn you on. The ubiquity of sexual images does not free eros but dilutes it.[25]

Many men think they will stop when they get married. But you're laying down patterns of behavior and thought that you'll take with you into your marriage. "It steadily got worse, even after I got married." "Sadly, this use has increased even since I've become a Christian and even since I've been married." "I thought married life would end the spiral of looking at porn, but I still looked at it once I got married."

Consider this: most porn addicts are married.[26] That reflects the fact that porn is not simply a substitute for sex. So don't be fooled. Many men have thought they would readily stop using porn when they got married. They were wrong. Don't think you're a special case.

Using porn is a bad way of preparing not to use it when you're married! Every time you use porn, you're giving it more control over your heart. You're sowing a bitter harvest for your married life. "Do not be deceived: God cannot be mocked. A man reaps what he sows. The one who sows to please his sinful nature, from that nature will reap destruction; the one who sows to please the Spirit, from the Spirit will reap eternal life" (Galatians 6:7-8).

6. PORN WRECKS FAMILIES

Studies show that even mild exposure to porn reduces men's evaluation of their partner's attractiveness and how much in love they feel.[27] It's harder to find satisfaction with real sex with real women. Porn is a cancer, eating away at your marriage and your enjoyment of marriage.

Porn also has the potential to end your marriage. "Porn wrecks marriages." That's the conclusion of divorce lawyer Marcia Maddox. Among the five lawyers in her office, there's always a case involving pornography being worked on at any given time. In one of her cases, a wife found out her husband was involved in Internet pornography while she and their daughter were working on a school project. The two were seated at the family computer together when suddenly a large window popped up depicting a giant penis ejaculating. . . . The couple wound up divorced, the mother awarded sole custody.[28]

Porn also endangers your children. More than one in ten men in my survey said they first encountered porn when they found their father's "secret" stash. It used to be magazines under a bed, but now it's the hard drive of your computer. Brian's story is typical: "I must confess that I struggle with pornography. I've done so for many years since finding some in my dad's office. I didn't even know what pornography was!" David writes, "The absolute worst point was when I went into a room and saw my dad on dodgy websites. That did two (contrasting) things. First, it made me think that what I did was OK. Second, it made me resent my dad because he made me think it was OK."

The effect on your children will be broader than this. Whether your children ever find it or not, porn will erode your moral authority within the home. You may fail to discipline them as you should because you feel a hypocrite. Or your discipline may be erratic and inconsistent, depending on how you recently you used porn.

Reasons 1 to 6 focused on the impact of porn on other people. Reasons 7 to 12 focus on its impact on us and our relationship to God and his people.

7. PORN IS ENSLAVING

"I kept resolving not to do it again," says Ahmed, "only to be out buying porn the next weekend. It felt like I needed to do it to relieve the desire and get it out of the system. Now I realize I was enslaved to it."

There's a law of diminishing returns with porn. "Studies on compulsive pornography use suggest that viewers habituate certain images and sex acts, and thus require more and more deviant materials to achieve sexual arousal."[29] It creates what psychologists call "tolerance"—we become so used to the images we see that they have less power to stimulate. We become desensitized. The result is that most porn users progressively look for more and more extreme images to get the same fix of pleasure.

Death and Destruction are never satisfied,
and neither are the eyes of man. (Proverbs 27:20)

Most people don't start out wanting to looking at anal sex, sadomasochistic sex and other forms of perversion. But that is where Internet porn takes you. Porn promises so much, but can't truly deliver, so it leaves you wanting more—more quantity and more extreme activity. Of the people in my survey, 94 percent had viewed hardcore porn (defined as porn depicting sexual acts) and over two-thirds had viewed porn depicting acts they would not consider appropriate within marriage.

Having my own home and unregulated Internet access was the start of my descent into viewing online porn. I started looking at naked images through Google, but over the next year or so got increasingly hooked. Softcore led to hardcore. Pictures were not enough, so I looked for video clips I could watch.

I found myself unable to stop looking at porn for long periods of time. My lust became harder to satisfy, and I looked for something different, frequently searching for porn featuring same-sex actors, nonconsensual sex or occasionally even pedophilia. At its worst, I would look at porn every day.

People often think that using porn provides an alternative to other sexual sins. "At least if he's looking at porn," many a wife has rationalized, "he won't be off with another woman." It's not true. Not only do porn users commonly move from softcore to hardcore images, but some move from online sex to real sex. Research shows that exposure to porn increases the likelihood of a person seeking out a prostitute. A number of stories I've heard bear out this trend: from pornography to strip clubs to prostitutes. When you click on your mouse you're not making a choice to visit a prostitute. But that is where that first click may eventually lead. Jack says, "It led to me having sexual encounters that I otherwise never would have had—things that were once unimaginable for me became less of a big deal." And Alyas writes:

> My spiritual life was so bad. I could never truly have communion with God the way he intended. . . . It caused me to sleep around with as many women as I could. I often had unprotected sex, because I would see it on the television and think it was OK. It led me to impregnate one of my former girlfriends and in the end we had an abortion, and I feel absolutely wretched for it.

Recently I heard of a Christian leader who was caught looking at child porn in an Internet café. The police were called, and now he faces a prison sentence. His marriage is wrecked, perhaps irretrievably. He has been in Christian ministry for more than thirty years. You don't think this could be you? He never thought porn would take over his life. He never started out with an interest in child porn. But porn gradually drew him deeper and deeper in.

8. PORN ERODES YOUR CHARACTER

Did King David decide one day to commit an act of murder? No. He was on the roof of his house and he let his eyes wander. And then his heart wandered. As a result, he committed adultery with Bathsheba. At this point he still had no thoughts of murder. But sin was *desensitizing* him. That's exactly the language Frank used to describe his use of porn to me: "It has desensitized me to sin and disobedience."

Speaking of lust, Jesus says, "If your right hand causes you to sin, cut it off and throw it away. It is better for you to lose one part of your body than for your whole body to go into hell" (Matthew 5:30). The words translated "causes you to sin" are used by Jesus elsewhere in

Matthew's Gospel to describe the person like seed sown on rocky ground who "falls away" when persecution comes (Matthew 13:21), and again, to describe in a time of persecution those who "will *turn away* from the faith and will betray and hate each other" (Matthew 24:10). The habit of sinning through lust does not end with lust. Left unchecked, it ends with falling away from Jesus.

In 1 Timothy 4:2 Paul talks about people "whose consciences have been seared as with a hot iron." They are people who've switched off their consciences so many times that they can't switch them on again. That's what porn will do to you. When you first use porn, you have to push past your conscience. Your conscience screams at you to stop. But you block your ears and close your heart. That's such a dangerous state to be in: walking around with ears blocked to the voice of God. Gradually you'll find it easier to use porn, as your conscience becomes a dull echo in the recesses of your heart. And soon your conscience will be too weak to warn you of other sins. The corrosion of porn will sweep into other areas of your life.

9. PORN WASTES YOUR TIME, ENERGY AND MONEY

"I've wasted hours at a time surfing through websites and blogs that show pornography." "At its height, I would turn to pornography multiple times a day." "I use porn three or four times a week for several hours at a time."

Think about a meal. You feel hungry, you consume the meal and then you feel satisfied. Twenty minutes later, you feel full and you don't want to eat any more. Think about porn. You feel a desire, you consume porn, but you don't feel satisfied. Porn doesn't deliver. Twenty minutes later, you still feel empty and you still want more.

Porn promises so much, but doesn't deliver. So you find yourself on an endless quest for the perfect image, the fulfilling scenario, another fix of the drug. Hours go by. A quick look becomes a wasted evening. You could have spent that time serving God, serving his people, reading the Bible, praying for mission, playing with your children or helping the broken. You could have spent that time connecting with your real wife in a real way. But you threw it away in front of a computer screen, all the time rotting your soul. It can never be recovered. It's an opportunity gone forever.

Or perhaps you start late at night, when everyone else is in bed, and you don't stop until two or three in the morning. Or you channel surf late in the evening, hoping for titillation that somehow (we tell ourselves) doesn't count as porn because it's on mainstream television. As a result, the next day becomes a write-off as far as any significant productive activity is concerned.

One of the "three As" that summarize the power of Internet porn is affordability. There's a lot of free porn on the Internet. But it's not so simple. The porn industry is not altruistic! It knows the addictive power of porn. It offers free porn to lure you into paid porn. The porn industry is larger than Microsoft, Google, eBay, Amazon, Yahoo and Apple *combined*. It makes money, and it makes that money from porn users.[30] Craig Gross tells the story of Steve, who has blown $20,000 on his addiction to porn,[31] while Richard Winter tells the story of a seminary student whose wife discovered a $400 bill for telephone sex.[32]

10. PORN WEAKENS YOUR RELATIONSHIP WITH GOD

King Solomon's reign was great. Not only did he build the temple, but the nations came to Israel to hear his wisdom, in partial fulfillment of God's promise that all nations would be blessed through his people. But his reign began to unravel because of his sexual sin. First Kings 11:1-2 tells us Solomon "loved many foreign women" and that he held fast to them "in love." It's the same word that's used in 1 Kings 3:3 to describe Solomon's love for God. Here is a love that rivals Solomon's love for God (cf. Deuteronomy 6:4-5). The writer interrupts the narrative to point out the dangers (1 Kings 11:2). The Israelites were not to marry foreign wives because "they will surely turn your hearts after their gods." And so it proves true in Solomon's life. "As Solomon grew old, his wives turned his heart after other gods, and his heart was not fully devoted to the LORD his God" (1 Kings 11:4).

Solomon's unchecked sexual desires turned his heart away from

God. They gave him a divided heart. "Porn kills my spiritual vitality and zaps the life out my personal devotional life and spiritual disciplines. It decreases my desire and consciousness of spiritual things, because it becomes the thing at the front of my mind, or more typically the guilt consumes me." "It has really deadened relationship with Jesus and robbed me of joy." "It definitely stopped me having a close relationship with God. I experienced such joy after stopping, and my prayer life has been reinvigorated."

Pete makes a perceptive comment: "One thing I've found when I'm struggling with pornography is that when I hear the word 'sin' I hear it to mean pornography." Imagine you're listening to a sermon. The preacher talks about the need to address sin in your life. There's only ever one sin that comes into your mind at that point: porn. And so you only ever address the issue of porn. The other sins of your heart go unaddressed. "Pornography stunts my growth in other areas," Pete concludes, "because I just don't notice them." He adds: "When I've had long periods without struggling I realize much more how sinful I am in other areas that I just don't notice when I'm struggling." The irony is that the sins that get ignored may well be the sins that underlie your use of porn.

Porn also robs you of your assurance of salvation. Again, the comments of people using porn tell the story. "It has led me to feel at times that I can't be loved by God. This is not only because of the depth of the sin itself, but also the regularity." "It makes me feel guilty and unworthy of his love, like he wouldn't want me in his family. I have felt ashamed to come before him and ask for his forgiveness at times—kind of like: 'I've done it again so he's not going to want to forgive me again!'" "My struggle with porn made me continually doubt my salvation. I knew I wasn't saved by works, but doubted how someone truly saved could habitually struggle."

11. PORN WEAKENS YOUR SERVICE

Joseph was a slave in Egypt in the household of a man called Potiphar. His abilities and faithfulness brought him to the attention of his master, and he was put in charge of the household. But he also came to the attention of Potiphar's wife. "He was well-built and handsome," the Bible says (Genesis 39:6). And so she gives him an invitation: "Come to bed with me." But Joseph refused. Day after day she pleaded with him, but day after day Joseph resisted. This is what he said:

> "With me in charge," he told her, "my master does not concern himself with anything in the house; everything he owns he has entrusted to my care. No one is greater in this house than I am. My master has withheld nothing from me except you, because you are his wife. How then could I do such a wicked thing and sin against God?" (Genesis 39:8-9)

Joseph is bound by his responsibility. He is obliged to keep the trust given him by Potiphar. He is loyal to a master who has treated him well. Above all, he is bound to a higher Master, against whom he will not sin. His responsibilities and his service are the reasons why he refuses to sin sexually.

Time and again, people talk about how porn has weakened their service of God.

> I feel that porn has done much harm to my service to my Savior and has prevented me from being more zealous and wholehearted about it.

> In terms of ministry the effect has been lost focus and lack of real life shining in the work I do—whether that's during church services or in relationships.

> The affect on my service has been devastating. It's one of the major reasons I've ended up giving up.

> I've been less able to serve Jesus as I was in effect living two lives. The stress of managing that kept me from being of any real use in the kingdom. I helped at a church youth group for around a year, but giving talks where I was meant to be sharing

about what God was doing in my life became too much of a strain, so I stopped.

This means *porn is a sin against your church*. Let's start at the most basic level. The time you spend using porn is time you could have spent serving your church. The tiredness you feel after staying up late affects your ability to serve others the following day.

But porn also corrodes your relationship with God, so that your service of others is impaired. If you feel distant from God, then you're distant from his grace, his love, his hope, his glory. Your motivation to serve is weakened and the divine resources you need may feel a long way away.

Or consider this. Will you ask challenging questions of your brothers if you've used porn in the last month? Probably not, because they might ask you questions in return.

In Joshua 7 the people of Israel attacked the town of Ai in their campaign to claim the Promised Land. Fresh from their remarkable success at Jericho, they took victory for granted. But they were routed and thirty-six men were killed. The reason? The secret sin of one man. Achan had hidden some of the spoils of victory that belonged to God. Nobody knew about Achan's sin, so it didn't act as a bad example to others. Yet it still corrupted the integrity of God's people and led to their defeat. Only when Achan and his sin were removed from God's people could they enjoy victory. No one may know about your use of porn. But it's still a sin against your church. It can still corrode God's people.

12. GOD'S WRATH IS AGAINST PEOPLE WHO USE PORN

One of the secrets of the power of porn is that it's secret. Anonymity is one of the "three As" that make cybersex so powerful. But porn is not anonymous. Often a wife will find out. And always God sees.

> The eyes of the LORD are everywhere,
>   keeping watch on the wicked and the good. (Proverbs 15:3)

> His eyes are on the ways of men;
>   he sees their every step. (Job 34:21)

Nothing in all creation is hidden from God's sight. Everything is uncovered and laid bare before the eyes of him to whom we must give account. (Hebrews 4:13)

And God's Word is unequivocal. God's wrath is against people who use porn:

But among you there must not be even a hint of sexual immorality, or of any kind of impurity, or of greed, because these are improper for God's holy people. Nor should there be obscenity, foolish talk or coarse joking, which are out of place, but rather thanksgiving. For of this you can be sure: No immoral, impure or greedy person—such a man is an idolater—has any inheritance in the kingdom of Christ and of God. Let no-one deceive you with empty words, for because of such things God's wrath comes on those who are disobedient. Therefore do not be partners with them. (Ephesians 5:3-7)

Don't let your good, sound theology of the perseverance of the saints deafen you to the awe-inducing warnings of Scripture:

If they have escaped the corruption of the world by knowing our Lord and Savior Jesus Christ and are again entangled in it and overcome, they are worse off at the end than they were at the beginning. It would have been better for them not to have known the way of righteousness, than to have known it and then to turn their backs on the sacred command that was passed on to them. (2 Peter 2:20-21)

Again and again God's Word warns against sexual sin, while celebrating sex. It's a beautiful and powerful thing that God intends to bind couples together in covenantal love. But its power for good can be corrupted.

Consider Proverbs 5. Here we find many of our reasons for avoiding porn echoed and summarized:

- Porn looks sweet, but leads to destruction (vv. 3-6).

- Porn wastes your time, energy and money (vv. 7-11).
- Porn leads to remorse and shame (vv. 12-14).
- Porn is a sin against your wife (vv. 15-20).
- Porn is a sin against the women involved and their husbands (v. 20).
- Porn may seem secret, but it is seen by God (v. 21).
- Porn is enslaving (v. 22).
- Porn leads to judgment (v. 23).

LOOKING BEYOND THE FRAME

When you look at porn, whether it's a still image or a movie, you need to look beyond the frame. Within the window you see a beautiful, smiling woman or a couple enjoying amazing sex. But think what's happening outside the frame. See the film crew gathered around. See the make-up artists, the plastic surgeons, the image editors. See the drugs and the suicides. Just off-screen there are women throwing up, taking drugs, committing suicide.

Look beyond the frame. See the warping of your view of sex, of your wife and of sisters in Christ. See the damage to your relationship with God and your service of his people. See God's wrath against your sin.

Look beyond the frame.

2

Freed by the Beauty of God

WHY DO PEOPLE USE PORN?

Time and again, people talk about the same triggers for porn:

- boredom

- exposure

- loneliness

- opportunity

- stress

- tiredness

- rejection

The following comments are typical: "The things that triggered it were tiredness, depression, loneliness and just not being able to stand up to the constant barrage of sexual imagery any more." "When I'm bored and alone—that's the number one trigger." "Tiny things trigger it. Usually images on the net or TV. Couple this with being alone and you have a bad combination." "Late at night. When family are out or in bed. Triggers are feelings of tiredness, loneliness and sexual frustration."

Occasionally the aftermath of a spiritual high can trigger a turning to porn. One person described how he would use porn after "a

really beneficial time spiritually—a conference or a mission." Another spoke of feeling "I was entitled to some spiritual low" after a
"spiritual high or mountain-top experience." When porn use becomes habitual your thoughts readily turn there, and then opportunity is all it takes to trigger temptation.

THE REASON FOR PORN

Being aware of the above can help guard against temptation. But none
of these triggers fully explains the place of porn in our lives.

Listen to the words of Jesus:

> For from within, out of men's hearts, come evil thoughts, sexual
> immorality, theft, murder, adultery, greed, malice, deceit, lewd-
> ness, envy, slander, arrogance and folly. All these evils come from
> inside and make a man "unclean." (Mark 7:21-23)

Where do evil thoughts, sexual immorality, adultery, lewdness come
from? From within, out of men's hearts. The circumstances of our
lives are significant. But they don't fully explain why we use porn.
After all, many people are tired and don't turn to porn. No: the Bible
teaches that the heart is the source of our behavior.

In the 1980s Gray Jolliffe and Peter Mayle created a cartoon series
called "Wicked Willie." Wicked Willie was a cartoon penis with a
mind of its own. Not only were the cartoons coarse, but more importantly they exemplified the idea that we're victims of our sex drive:
"It was my willy what made me do it."

People sometimes objectify the penis, seeing it as an "other" we
can blame for our sexual behavior. In the modern worldview, desire
and will are often seen to be in opposition. We fail when our desires
are too strong for our will, or when our will is too weak to resist. The
porn user becomes a victim of his own desires: "My willy made me
do it." This reflects a dualism in modern thinking in which mind and
body are two separate entities battling against each other: "I'm a victim of my own body with its sexual urges" (which are seen as separate from "me").

But in the biblical view of humanity, desire drives the will. I do what I want to do. The source of my behavior is my heart. "Above all else," says Proverbs 4:23, "guard your heart, for it is the wellspring of life." In other words, the heart is the fountain or source of my conduct.

Western culture uses the heart to refer to our emotions. But in the Bible the heart represents my essential self. I feel with my heart, but I also think with my heart. I fear, long, love, hope, decide with my heart. Where my heart leads, my behavior follows.

If we don't blame our willy, then sometimes we blame our wives. We've seen that there is evidence to suggest that using porn causes men to show less interest in marital sex and become worse at true sexual intimacy. But it's a mistake to think that the causation works in the opposite direction: that a lack of sex or "poor" sex with your wife leads to porn use. Porn is never simply a substitute for sex. Indeed, there's a sense in which sex is the one thing porn doesn't offer—not real sex. Your wife may not act like a porn star, but then neither does the porn star—not in real life. Porn is not offering you a real experience of sex. It's offering a fantasy substitute for power or success or worship or reward. The problem doesn't lie with your wife, but in your heart. To blame your wife is a form of spiritual abuse—you're transferring the blame for your sin to her; imposing a false guilt on her.[1] "Out of men's hearts," says Jesus, "come evil thoughts, sexual immorality."

Or we blame our history. We claim, "My parents made me do it." Again, there's good evidence that parental relationships have a profound effect on the way people express themselves sexually. Demanding parents who offered little nurture can create a desire to perform that becomes sexualized. We've seen that women caught up in the sex industry commonly experienced an absent father. Sexual abusers were themselves often abused as children. This evidence reminds us of the crucial importance of good parenting. These factors shape people's lives and increase the power of sexual temptation in their lives. But they do not provide a complete explanation for sinful behavior.

When tempted, no one should say, "God is tempting me." For God cannot be tempted by evil, nor does he tempt anyone; but each one is tempted when, by his own evil desire, he is dragged away and enticed. Then, after desire has conceived, it gives birth to sin; and sin, when it is full-grown, gives birth to death. (James 1:13-15)

We can't blame our sin on the circumstances God has allowed in our lives. They may be massive factors, but they're not sufficient causes. James says the ultimate cause of sin is our "own evil desire."

James's words are important for those who claim that porn is the result of a "spirit of lust" in a person's life. There is no biblical evidence to suggest that demons can inhabit a child of God. The Holy Spirit does not cohabit! Certainly Satan tempts us to sin. Peter says:

Be self-controlled and alert. Your enemy the devil prowls around like a roaring lion looking for someone to devour. Resist him, standing firm in the faith, because you know that your brothers throughout the world are undergoing the same kind of sufferings. (1 Peter 5:8-9)

We are fools if we don't take this seriously. But we don't resist the devil through some kind of exorcizing prayer. We do so by being "self-controlled and alert," "standing firm in the faith," by avoiding temptation and countering it with the belief that God offers more than sin. James 1 reminds us that, while Satan can use the enticements of the world to tempt us, we can't blame the devil. We can't say, "The demons made me do it." Satan is powerful, but even Satan is not the ultimate cause of sin in our lives. James goes on to tell us to "resist the devil" by coming near to God in humility and repentance (James 4:7-10).

Take a moment to read David's response to his sexual sin in Psalm 51. See if you can detect any trace of David blaming his sex drive or his parents or his circumstances or the devil. Where does David place responsibility for his sin? Where does he place his hope for the future?

TAKING RESPONSIBILITY

So circumstances often trigger our sin and shape the form it takes, but they don't cause it. The root cause is always our hearts and their sinful desires. We sin because we believe lies about God, instead of believing God's Word, and because we worship idols instead of worshiping God.[2]

If the problem were simply with our eyes, then the solution would be to avert our eyes. But if the problem begins in the heart, then the solution must be much more fundamental. So you need to ask yourself: When do I turn to porn? What's going on in my heart when I turn to porn?

You might find it helpful to keep a journal. When are you tempted? What's happening in the rest of your life when you're tempted? How are you feeling? What's on your mind? This may help you to see what's going on when you struggle. You may begin to see what porn "provides" for you. Does it offer an escape? Is it an act of revenge? Is it a way of feeling powerful or loved or wanted? Is it a reward you give to yourself?

You can then begin to identify the false promises that porn makes to you. And then you can also identify the liberating truth of the gospel that can begin to set you free.

FREED BY FAITH

This is love for God: to obey his commands. And his commands are not burdensome, for everyone born of God overcomes the world. This is the victory that has overcome the world, even our faith. Who is it that overcomes the world? Only he who believes that Jesus is the Son of God. . . .

And this is the testimony: God has given us eternal life, and this life is in his Son. He who has the Son has life; he who does not have the Son of God does not have life. (1 John 5:3-5, 11-12)

We can defeat porn. We have victory. There is hope. You don't need to feel defeated. How do we have victory? Through our faith (v. 4); through believing Jesus is the Son of God. This is where many of us have gone wrong. We've tried to find victory through our own effort.

Belief in the Son brings eternal life. This means life rather than the empty existence of sin. Peter says we "were redeemed from the empty way of life handed down to you from your forefathers" (1 Peter 1:18). Jesus gives real life—a full life, life with meaning—in the place of an empty life. And belief in the Son brings eternal life. Hebrews says, "the pleasures of sin [are] for a short time" (Hebrews 11:25). By contrast, Psalm 16:11 says:

> You have made known to me the path of life;
>   you will fill me with joy in your presence,
>   with eternal pleasures at your right hand.

How does faith in Jesus lead to victory over porn? Faith sees through the false promises of porn, sees that God offers more than porn and sees that God is always bigger and better than porn. So faith chooses God, worships God, treasures God, adores God.

"Suppose I am tempted to lust," says John Piper. "The power of all temptation is the prospect that it will make me happier. No one sins out of a sense of duty." So what should I do? Plenty of people say it's a question of the will; but, says Piper, people who strive for moral improvement can't say, "The life I live I live . . . *by faith*" (Galatians 2:20). So how do we fight lust by faith?

> When faith has the upper hand in my heart I am satisfied with Christ and his promises. This is what Jesus meant when he said, "He who *believes* in me shall *never thirst*" (John 6:35). When my thirst for joy and meaning and passion are satisfied by promsies of Christ, the power of sin is broken.[3]

PORN IS ALWAYS A SYMPTOM OF UNBELIEF AND IDOLATRY

Psalm 51 is the prayer of David "when the prophet Nathan came to him after David had committed adultery with Bathsheba." You'll find the background story in 2 Samuel 11–12. Psalm 51 is a powerful prayer of confession that, over the years, many Christians have made their own. But have you ever noticed that it makes no mention of sex? It's a prayer of confession after an act of adultery, but there's no mention of that adultery. Indeed, David says to God:

> Against you, you only, have I sinned
> and done what is evil in your sight,
> so that you are proved right when you speak
> and justified when you judge. (Psalm 51:4)

Clearly, David had sinned against Bathsheba, against her husband and against his other wives. But first and foremost, he had sinned against God. Your porn is a sin against your wife, against women and against the church. But above all, it is a sin against God.

The early theologian Augustine saw himself as a sex addict. He wrote in his autobiographical *Confessions*, "From a perverse will came lust, and slavery to lust became a habit, and the habit, being constantly yielded to, became a necessity and they held me fast in a hard slavery." Looking back, he recognized that this slavery was a reflection of his hunger for God: "I was seeking you outside myself, and finding not the God of my heart."[4] G. K. Chesterton said: "Every man who knocks on the door of a brothel is looking for God."[5]

> Among you there must not be even a hint of sexual immorality, or of any kind of impurity, or of greed, because these are improper for God's holy people. . . . For of this you can be sure: No immoral, impure or greedy person—such a man is an idolater—has any inheritance in the kingdom of Christ and of God. (Ephesians 5:3-5)

A man who is immoral, impure or greedy "is an idolater." The context makes it clear that the writer is talking about sexual immorality and greed for sex. Sexual sin is an act or sign of idolatry. Something matters more to us than God. We desire, want, treasure, worship something in God's place. David White of Harvest USA says, "Sexual sin is not primarily about lust. . . . It is first and foremost a violation of the first Great Commandment, an idol that replaces the Creator. This means in the face of frustration, loneliness, anxiety, stress, etc. the individual runs to a false god."[6]

WHAT PORN OFFERS AND HOW GOD OFFERS MORE

"It was a surface issue," says Martin of his porn, "for deeper unresolved issues of sin." David Powlison of the Christian Counseling and Educational Foundation says,

> It's easy for your big, obvious sins (like surfing the Internet for pornographic material) to conceal the deeper sins that fuel your struggle with pornography. But unless you recognize and repent of the sin patterns underlying your addiction, you won't be fighting the right battle.[7]

Asked for his advice to fellow strugglers, Ian says, "Focus on the reason why you look at porn. Discover why these reasons are empty, promising much but delivering little. Discover what the good news means for you in this respect."

So what are the underlying promises of porn? We're going to continue looking at six false promises of porn. Not every theme will be true for you, but most porn users will identify with one or two themes, and there will be some overlap. They're a simplification to help you identify why you turn to porn and how you can turn from porn to God.

So with every false promise of porn there is a true promise of God. Whatever porn offers, God offers more. It's this truth that sets us free (John 8:31-36). "In God's mercy," says Trevor, "he's shown me that the promises of porn are hollow lies. In his incomprehensible sovereignty, God has used my weaknesses to make me cling to and rejoice in Christ—the fulfilment of all his promises." "God is far more fulfilling than porn," says Pete, "I've tried both and, as crazy as it sounds to someone neck-deep in using porn, God is way more satisfying."

So our second key ingredient in the battle against porn, the central ingredient, is this: *an adoration of God—a desire for God arising from a confidence that he offers more than porn.*

Table 2. Second Key Ingredient in the Battle Against Porn

1	abhorence of porn	a hatred of porn itself (not just the shame it brings) and a longing for change
2	adoration of God	a desire for God, arising from a confidence that he offers more than porn
3	assurance of grace	an assurance that you are loved by God and right with God through faith in the work of Jesus
4	avoidance of temptation	a commitment to do all in your power to avoid temptation, starting with controls on your computer
5	accountability to others	a community of Christians who are holding you accountable and supporting you in your struggle

HOLLOW PROMISES, REAL PROMISES

Porn Promises Respect.
Porn creates a fantasy world in which I am potent. We use the word *potent* to describe both power and sexual ability. It shows how closely the two correlate in our minds and culture. Sexual prowess is a symbol of power. A sex addict, says Craig Lockwood, "thinks of his sexual performance, and the attractiveness of his body, as an indicator and a measure of his worth and adequacy."[8] In my fantasy world I can perform. Indeed, I'm worshiped for my performance. Porn offers an opportunity to reimagine ourselves as sex gods worthy of respect. If porn offers you respect, then accompanying fantasies are likely to involve one or more of the following: increased staying power, situations in which you are dominant, better sexual performance than other people, an impressive body and multiple partners.

"For most men," says Robert Jensen, "it starts with the soft voice that speaks to our deepest fear: That we aren't man enough. . . . Sex is sexy because men are dominant and women are subordinate; power is eroticized."[9] "The trigger for me is rejection," says Brian. "I turn to porn when I lack confidence. Instead of seeking to fill myself with God, I believe that sin can fill me up." "It made me feel excited and manly," says Pete. Another Christian who's struggled with porn put it like this:

This sense of unworthiness may drive someone to be the sort of person who looks very different from a sex addict. They may be outstanding performers in life: popular, good humored and successful people; leaders in church; businessmen; sporting achievers. But their successes are driven by the secret suspicion that no one would really like them if they were genuinely known by others for who they really are.[10]

This perhaps goes some way to explaining why porn is so often a problem for church leaders. Three factors combine. First, there is a pressure toward self-justification—to prove you're a good leader or worth your salary. Porn provides a fantasy world in which you're potent, adored, appreciated. It creates the illusion of self-justification. Second, this is coupled with maximum opportunity. Many men work all day and then spend their evenings surrounded by their family, so opportunities are limited. But church leaders are alone for large proportions of their week, sitting in front of high-speed Internet access. Porn is just a click away. Third, many church leaders feel unable to talk to anyone. People expect them to be examples of godliness. Many fear they'll lose their jobs if they tell anyone. Perhaps they will. And so they hide in the dark, and the dark is a breeding ground for porn.

One version of "porn as respect" is "porn as rejuvenation." For some men porn is part of a mid-life crisis. It's the secret version of an affair with a younger woman. It might be about the man feeling his mortality, or questioning his achievements in life, or feeling he no longer has a "perfect" body. And so we strike out for youth by "having" a younger woman. We enter a world where we and the objects of our sexual desire are young.

God Is Glorious—He Is the One We Should Fear.

In the fantasy world of porn, people respect me, admire me, accept me. Women "offer" themselves to me. I project myself onto the stud and vicariously experience his potency. I'm impressive, respected, worshiped by men. But it's all artificial.

God offers genuine acceptance. We're desperate to prove or justify ourselves, but we can't. We're not good enough, not man enough, not adequate enough—not for God. But God graciously accepts us in Christ, justifying us through Christ. We need the humility to accept—and the faith to find—confidence in Christ.

But perhaps the real issue is that God's acceptance is not enough. What we really want is the approval of other people, in this case often the approval of other men. In biblical terms, our porn is driven by the fear of man. The answer is the fear of the Lord. He is the glorious One, whose opinion should matter. And he's the One whose approval we already have in Christ.

Porn Promises Relationship.

We crave intimacy at a relational level. We feel lonely. But we also fear intimacy. We're not sure we can attain it or be vulnerable enough to handle it. "The sex addict learns to medicate this sense of isolation and unworthiness with pornography."[11] Porn offers a safe alternative to intimacy.

> Porn provided the fantasy of an intimate yet passionate relationship. It seemed like a safe way to be sexually active without getting involved in a real relationship.

> I used it because it made me feel less lonely. I tended to use live-camera chatrooms, where I could have a private conversation with someone who was pleased to see me and who would make me feel good.

> Mostly, it satisfies for me a sense of acceptance and love. This isn't something I think about consciously, but I know it's the root issue.

> It seems to provide a false intimacy—a woman showing you something that is private. Part of me feels lucky to have been allowed to see what I'm seeing.

It offers a deep sense of intimacy when I feel alone and over-whelmed. It takes a lot more work to talk to God, my wife or another person than it does to look at porn.

In "porn as respect" we want to be respected by men. In "porn as relationship" we want to be worshiped or desired by women. Accompanying fantasies may include some elements in common with "porn as respect" but with a focus on impressing women rather than out-performing men: a desirable body, staying power, multiple partners or multiple orgasms for your partner.

Or we want to be sovereign over women. We fear women, intimacy and losing control. Our fantasies don't replicate the reality of our lives but offer a safe alternative. We enact what we lack the courage or ability to do in real life. We're cowards who wish we were heroes. "It made me feel better about myself," says Greg. "I had control. I could see a naked woman any time I wanted!" George says porn for him was about "having that sense of ownership over the woman." And so we look at images in which the man is in control. Robert Jensen quotes a porn user who acknowledges:

> For me, porn is all about *controlling human beings*, or I should say the illusion of controlling others. That's what got me off. I felt so out of control in my life and from my childhood, that this was something I could control (which women I would see naked or I could hit the pause button and extend a particular image for eternity for example). There is no vulnerability, no risk, and therefore, no growth. I think that for me, the illusion of control-ling women, even in masturbatory porn fantasies, was a mis-guided attempt to quell the fear that I have around women.[12]

Another form of this is viewing so-called lesbian sex. I say "so-called" because it doesn't actually involve lesbians, nor is it designed for consumption by lesbians, but involves (usually otherwise hetero-sexual) women pleasuring each other for men to watch. This is risk-free intimacy. I'm not involved. Two women are available to me, but at no risk.

God Is Great—He Is Sovereign over Our Relationships.

If "porn as respect" is driven by the fear of man, then "porn as relationship" is driven by the fear of woman (or the fear of man, if you're a woman). Fearing rejection, we retreat into the fantasy world of porn in which women adore us and offer themselves to us without risk. But again, this is an artificial world.

Life is full of risk. Trusting God doesn't take that risk away. People might still reject us. But trusting God takes some risks away. We can be confident that "in all things God works for the good of those who love him, who have been called according to his purpose" (Romans 8:28). God will use the events of our life—including the failed relationships—to conform us "to the likeness of his Son" (Romans 8:29). And conformity to Christ is what matters most.

When we're tempted to turn to porn, we need to think of God as our heavenly Father. We need to rest in his sovereign care, not replace it with a pretend sovereignty. We need to tell ourselves, "God is in control, and God is good to me." "Cast all your anxiety on him because he cares for you" (1 Peter 5:7).

There'll be times when you're hurt by members of the opposite sex. There'll be times when you are frustrated by your own fears. But don't opt for a pretend intimacy.

Porn Promises Refuge.

"Porn served as a stress reliever," says Geoff, "when I should be relying on Christ as my source of rest and strength." For many people, porn is a place of refuge. It's a form of escapism to which they turn when they feel overwhelmed or defeated. "I use pornography mainly to escape responsibilities that seem too much for me to handle," says George. He's not alone. "Most often I went to porn when life or ministry got overwhelming. Porn became a means of escape." "It's escapism; I pretend I'm a different person, with a different life where I'm not in control and have no responsibilities." "I use it to relieve frustration. It gives me a perfect world of sex. I feel strong, dominant. I don't believe God is a better substitute."

Perhaps you're facing a big, daunting task. Or perhaps you're facing a difficulty at work or in your marriage. Or perhaps you fear failure. Instead of taking responsibility, you turn to porn. You enter a fantasy world in which you're successful. Here's a world in which you're adored, in control, where success is guaranteed. "Porn is my own little world," says Oliver. Porn becomes the way we medicate our negative feelings rather than taking them to God.

The act of looking at porn is itself part of the succour it purports to offer. I can search for women who are all available to me. I can choose between them like some sovereign being. It offers a sense of control.

One specific version of this, albeit one that's less common, is where men want a dominatrix. Often, these are men with roles involving a high level of responsibility. The dominatrix offers them a complete abdication of responsibility. They can give up entirely any decision making and instead allow themselves to be told what to do. They leave behind the responsibilities of being the boss and choose temporary servitude.

Porn creates its own vicious circle. You turn to porn for refuge, and using porn gives you a brief high. But that's followed by a big low of shame and guilt, so you turn again to porn for refuge.

Gordon MacDonald identifies three cultural stereotypes that shape our sense of what it means to be a man:

- A real man is a hunter and provider: he fears failure.

- A real man is a stud: he fears rejection.

- A real man is a fighter: he fears powerlessness.[13]

It's not difficult to see how porn feeds off these cultural expectations. It creates a fantasy that perfectly matches each of these fears. If you fear failure, then porn promises success—you always get the woman. If you fear rejection, then porn promises approval—a woman worships you. If you fear powerlessness, then porn promises potency—women are under your power, whether they are overpowered by your sexual allure or, in more extreme porn, by your physical dominance.

God Is Great—He Is Sovereign over Our Lives.

For some, porn is a place of refuge, an escape when life seems too much. Consider David's response to such pressures in Psalm 18:1-3:

> I love you, O LORD, my strength.
> The LORD is my rock, my fortress and my deliverer;
>   my God is my rock, in whom I take refuge.
> He is my shield and the horn of my salvation, my
>   stronghold.
> I call to the LORD, who is worthy of praise,
>   and I am saved from my enemies.

David sang this song "when the LORD delivered him from the hand of all his enemies and from the hand of Saul." Was David under pressure! He was looking for an escape. So he turned to the Lord. He describes God as "my rock, my fortress, my deliverer, my refuge, my shield, my salvation, my stronghold." Find comfort in these descriptions of God.

David goes on to describe how God comes to his aid:

> The earth trembled and quaked,
>   and the foundations of the mountains shook; . . .
> He parted the heavens and came down; . . .
> The LORD thundered from heaven,
>   the voice of the Most High resounded. (Psalm 18:7, 9, 13).

Here is someone more powerful than any of our circumstances. Think of the pressures you face—and then put them side by side in your mind with this thundering, fire-breathing God.

What does this powerful God do when he arrives?

> He reached down from on high and took hold of me;
>   he drew me out of deep waters.
> He rescued me from my powerful enemy,
>   from my foes, who were too strong for me.
> They confronted me in the day of my disaster,
>   but the LORD was my support.

He brought me out into a spacious place;
   he rescued me because he delighted in me. (Psalm 18:16-19)

God reaches down and holds us. He's there to support us. Imagine
yourself lifted to that spacious place, delighting in God and enjoying
his delight in you. Surely this is a far better place than the sordid,
false world of porn!

Next time you're tempted to medicate your emotions with porn,
take your problems to God. "Humble yourselves, therefore, under
God's mighty hand, that he may lift you up in due time. Cast all your
anxiety on him because he cares for you" (1 Peter 5:6-7).

Porn Promises Reward.
"It's a bit of well-deserved pleasure. I turn to porn instead of God
because the short-term thrill is different to what God provides in that
moment." "I used it as an escape from reality. Reality was good at the
time, but I was restless and living a dull, uninteresting life." "Sometimes I felt I deserved it, especially if my wife was not in the mood. I
loved the sensation, the high, the excitement."

It's common for porn users to turn to porn when life is dull or hard
or disappointing. Or after deadlines, exams, preaching—after a period of intense work or self-denial. Porn is a reward: "I deserve this."
There is often what Mark Laaser calls an "entitlement factor." Many
men minimize the sin because they feel themselves overworked and
underappreciated.[14] Have you found yourself thinking something
like this: *I'm always doing things for other people, but no one does anything for me?* Or *I'm giving up stuff for Christ—a well-paid job or sex—
so now it's my turn?*

God Is Good—He Is Our Ultimate and Lasting Joy.
Many people turn to porn because it's pleasurable. Porn is a reward
they've earned for their hard work. Or simply a quick fix. And porn
is pleasurable and offers its pleasure quickly. But then what? Its leg-
acy is emptiness, guilt, shame.

Jesus promises the Samaritan woman he met at the well living water that would truly satisfy (John 4). Then he asks her to fetch her husband. The words look like a strange tangent, but they lead straight to her heart. Jesus knows she's had five husbands, and the man she's with now is not her husband. This woman has been looking for meaning, satisfaction and fulfillment in marriage, sex and intimacy. But they're like water that leaves her thirsty again. No doubt there was pleasure. But it didn't last. It wasn't the real thing. It left her wanting more.

She tries to change the subject with a question about where we worship, but Jesus uses it to go right to the heart of the issue. What matters is not *where* you worship but *what* you worship. She was trying to find satisfaction from a man instead of from God and in the process made an idol of sexual intimacy. But the math tells the story: five husbands, plus another man. The math of your porn habit tells its own story as well. It shows what you've been looking to porn to provide, and it has not delivered.

To paraphrase John 4:13-14: "Everyone who drinks the water of porn will be thirsty again, but whoever drinks the water Jesus gives him will never thirst. Indeed, the water Jesus gives him will become in him a spring of water welling up to eternal life." This living water is God himself, communicated to his people through the Holy Spirit (John 7:37-39). Our longing for porn is a version of our longing for God. Susan says, "There've been times in my life when I've been so hungry for God that all I did was fast and pray with my friends—and utterly forgot about masturbating for about two years."

One of our problems is that we think only of moments. In the moment we think the pleasures of sin are real and the joy of God is insubstantial or distant. But in truth it's the other way round: every joy we experience is but a shadow of the source of all joy, which is God. C. S Lewis famously said: "There have been times when I think we do not desire heaven; but more often I find myself wondering whether, in our heart of hearts, we have ever desired anything else. . . . It is the secret signature of each soul, the incommunicable and unappeasable want."[15] The life of obedience is not the bad life or a sad life. It's the good life. Life with God and for God is the best life you could live. Change is about enjoying the freedom from sin and the delight in God that God gives to us through Jesus.

Boredom is a common reason cited for turning to porn. But is it really a reason? Consider this: why not turn to the Bible or prayer instead? OK, I'm not naive! I know the answer. The Bible and prayer don't seem much fun. Porn is easy pleasure. Reading Scripture and spending time in prayer are routes to true and lasting joy in Christ. But we don't take that path because we want quick and easy pleasure. In other words, boredom is not the issue, but laziness is. We want our pleasure now and we want it without any effort.

Or maybe the problem is that we don't really believe that the effort will be worthwhile. *So what if I read my Bible and pray for an hour? Is that really going to give me the buzz of porn?* We lack the faith to find joy in God. We opt for cheap pleasures over lasting pleasure because we lack faith. Compare this with Moses. Moses had access to all the luxuries of Egypt, but he gladly gave them up because he had faith in the treasure of Christ.

> By faith Moses, when he had grown up, refused to be known as the son of Pharaoh's daughter. He chose to be ill-treated along with the people of God rather than to enjoy the pleasures of sin for a short time. He regarded disgrace for the sake of Christ as of greater value than the treasures of Egypt, because he was looking ahead to his reward. (Hebrews 11:24-26)

Porn Promises Revenge.

Porn can be an expression of anger, revenge, resentment or ingratitude. It may be an act against your wife, perhaps when sex is not forthcoming. Andy concedes he turns to porn "if I feel in any way hard done by my wife's provision of actual sex!" "The wife and I will argue," explains Bill, "and I'll let it fester, and when I'm on my own I'll let my eyes wander online." Tyrone says, "I used porn as an expression of my frustration that I wasn't having sex with my wife more often. I thought on some level that it 'served her right' for not being more interested in me."

Or porn may be an act of anger against God, when life hasn't turned out the way we want. We might not have the honesty to say it out loud, but in our hearts we think, *If God is treating me like this then I don't see why I should bother with his ideals.* "I become frustrated with God," says Gordon, "that he's made me a sexual being and yet I have no allowed outlet for this part of who I am." Dr. Mark Laaser believes anger is a common reason Christian men commit sexual sin. "They are angry at God, angry at their spouse, angry at church," he says. "They feel abandoned."[16]

David Powlison describes counseling Tom, who had struggled with pornography since he was a teenager. He'd tried all the right things, but still he struggled. When Powlison asked him to keep a record of the times he was tempted, Tom said, "I already know when. It's usually on Friday night. It's my temper tantrum with God." On Friday nights, Tom thinks of his friends out on dates or with their wives. "I feel sorry for myself. I get angry at God because I think he owes me a wife." "I thought his big struggle was with pornography," comments Powlison, "but all of a sudden he was talking about anger at God! . . . Tom was a legalist. He believed that when he tried to be a good Christian God owed him goodies (such as a wife), and when he did something wrong he despaired."[17]

God Is Gracious—He Gives Us More Than We Deserve.

In some ways "porn as revenge" is a version of "porn as reward." We can think that we deserve porn because of what we've endured or given up. The twist with "porn as revenge" is that we feel someone isn't giving us what we deserve. We're angry with our wives for not giving us the sex we want. Or we're angry with God for not giving us the life we want. Indeed, anger toward our wives reflects an unspoken—perhaps unrecognized—anger at God for not giving us the wife or the sex we want.

It reflects a contractual view of our relationship with God. We do things for God or we give up things for God and we have a right to certain blessings in return. If God doesn't deliver on his side of the bargain, we're justified in no longer keeping our side. We have a right to be angry toward God and a right to take revenge: a right to porn.

But God doesn't treat us on a contractual basis. He treats us according to grace. He doesn't give us what we deserve: he gives us more than we deserve. He gives us what Christ deserves. In a sense God does treat us on the basis of a contract—the covenant he makes with his people through the blood of Christ. But this is a covenant of grace. What we deserve from God is his wrath, but what we get is the righteousness of Christ.

A contractual view of God is the attitude of the elder brother in the parable of the prodigal son. "He answered his father, 'Look! All these years I've been slaving for you and never disobeyed your orders. Yet you never gave me even a young goat so I could celebrate with my friends' " (Luke 15:29). He's angry because he doesn't think that his work has been rewarded. But the heart of the issue is revealed in the phrase "all these years I've been slaving for you." He thinks of himself as a slave rather than a son. "'My son,' the father said, 'you are always with me, and everything I have is yours'" (v. 31).

Do you think of yourself as a slave of God? Then no wonder you turn to porn in anger to get what you think you deserve. But we're not God's slaves. We're his sons and daughters. If God doesn't give us the partner or the sex or the success we long for, it's because he knows best because he has a bigger agenda, because he's making us like his Son, because he wants us to long for the real treasure of knowing him. Marriage or sex or success has become an idol in our hearts. When we can't have it, we feel bitter toward God, because it matters more to us than God. God is prying our fingers away from it so we can grasp hold of him and the greater treasure that is already ours in Christ. You may not have a spouse or great sex or success or a lot of other things. But you do have the living God. "My son, my daughter, you are always with me, and everything I have is yours."

Porn Promises Redemption.
For some people, porn offers redemption, in terms of acceptance and affirmation, an alternative righteousness. "I just want to feel that I'm OK. I turn to porn instead of God because the gospel doesn't tell me that I'm OK. It tells me I'm a wicked sinner and Jesus died in my place. The gospel demands that I change. Porn says, 'You're OK just as you are.'" "Why not God? Time with God is laden with all sorts of complicated emotions and thoughts, and doesn't evoke the same strength of 'lift.'"

For others porn offers a form of redemption through self-atonement. Porn is the punishment they inflict on themselves to redeem themselves. In "porn as revenge," my anger is directed against God or my wife. But in "porn as redemption" my anger is directed against myself. I feel a strong sense of self-loathing and turn to porn to confirm this verdict. "I turn to porn instead of God," says Kurt, "because often I feel God has rejected me." I play the shameful role I assign to myself. It becomes an act of self-harm akin to taking a sharp object to your arm. "I guess I had a very distorted view of God at the time. I felt like I had to tick lots of boxes to make myself presentable to God, and I knew I had nothing good within me. Porn was a way of escaping from God, in a sense, but it only made me feel worse."

Pastor Rob Bell says:

> Lust always wants more. Which is why lust, over time, will always lead to despair. Which will always lead to anger. . . . Sometimes it isn't expressed on the outside because it turns inwards. That's depression. When it goes outward, it will often affect what a person indulges in—darker and darker expressions of unfulfilled desire mixed with contempt. Is that how someone ends up at leather and whips?[18]

This is anger at self, but it's also pride toward God. I'm too proud to accept his pardoning grace. I need to self-atone. And so I wallow in self-pity and self-loathing. If this is how porn works for you, then you'll hate porn but still need it. It provides something for you—a sense of redemption, of self-atonement. It confirms your verdict on yourself and enacts judgment against your guilty self.

God Is Gracious—He Is the One Who Atones for Our Sin.

I waited patiently for the LORD;
    he turned to me and heard my cry.
He lifted me out of the slimy pit,
    out of the mud and mire;
he set my feet on a rock
    and gave me a firm place to stand.
He put a new song in my mouth,
    a hymn of praise to our God. (Psalm 40:1-3)

Porn is a window onto your heart. It's where you go when left to yourself. But God is gracious. We don't have to remain in the pit of porn. We can look to God to lift us out, to give us a firm place, a good place, with a new song. We don't have to wallow in self-pity—we can sing hymns of praise to our God.

Don't choose the pit. Don't let porn shape your identity. God calls us his sons and daughters. Trust the finished work of Christ, who died to give you a new life. When you're tempted to wallow in porn, remember this: "I have been crucified with Christ and I no longer live, but Christ lives in me. The life I live in the body, I live by faith in the Son of God, who loved me and gave himself for me" (Galatians 2:20). Your old identity has been crucified; it's dead and gone. Its habits of thought and behavior may linger on, but it no longer defines you. You can embrace a new life, lived by faith in the Son of God. You're loved. And this is the measure of Christ's love for you: he gave himself for you.

Day after day every priest stands and performs his religious duties; again and again he offers the same sacrifices, which can never take away sins. But when this priest had offered for all time one sacrifice for sins, he sat down at the right hand of God. Since that time he waits for his enemies to be made his footstool, because by one sacrifice he has made perfect forever those who are being made holy. (Hebrews 10:11-14)

The priests offered sacrifices again and again because they could never atone for sin. Perhaps that's how you feel: day in, day out, you must atone for your sin. Again and again you must suffer: wallowing in porn, harming yourself with destructive behavior. But Jesus our great High Priest has "offered for all time one sacrifice for sin." And then he sat down—a sign that his work was done. "It is finished." There's nothing left to do. Christ has paid the price of your porn in full. "By one sacrifice he has made perfect forever those who are being made holy." You're being made holy, and perhaps you feel keenly the ongoing strain of your sin. But in God's sight you're perfect, through the perfect work of Christ. Listen to Peter's testimony:

I knew I'd earned condemnation and guilt. When I finally saw Jesus taking that guilt on himself for me I was horrified and amazed that he would do that for me. I came to understand his love in a way I'd never have known had I not been so lost and needy for salvation. My struggle with porn caused me to re-evaluate the legalistic, graceless God of my youth.

THE FIGHT OF FAITH

"I don't want Jesus to break the cycle of porn," Bob told me, "because I'm afraid Jesus will be a poor substitute." Bob is not alone.

I use it instead of turning to God because it's so readily available, and in that moment God doesn't seem to be near, even though I know he is.

I turn to it because it appeals more to my senses than God does in those moments. It feels like it has more power over me than God in those moments.

The only reason I didn't turn to God instead was that I didn't believe he was really satisfying and complete for what I need. I believed the lies of Genesis 3 all over again.

It is easier to turn to porn than God.

Let no one suggest that turning from the false promises of porn to the promise of God is easy. Faith in Jesus is not a quick fix. It's certainly not a case of "just believe." There's no "just" about it. Yes, the message is "believe." But it's never "*just* believe." We're called to the fight of faith. So instead of "just believe," the message is "fight to believe." And it will be a fight, a daily fight. Some days you'll be wounded; some days you'll lose the battle. Then you'll have to pick yourself up, fight to believe in God's grace and reenter the fray.

Ron says, "I remind myself that porn will not make me happy and fulfill me but just make me feel more empty. I remind myself that Christ fulfills. He is better and leads to more joy. I just don't have enough strength, sometimes." That's biblical realism. There's the fight to believe that Christ fulfills; that Christ is better than porn. And sometimes we lose the fight. But the battle goes on. How did change take place for Pete? "I 'manned' up! I realized the depravity of it all in light of a higher, weightier gospel. I believed in the promises of God more than the promises of porn."

This is why so many people speak of turning to porn when they're tired. It's not because they think porn will be a pick-me-up—otherwise they'd make themselves a coffee instead. It's because they don't feel they have the energy for the fight of faith. It requires discipline. George says, "The temptations will come when I'm feeling down and tired. However, through rejoicing in the gospel at the start of each day, I'm winning the fight." It's when we're tired that more than ever we need companions—other Christians to stand with us in the fight and, above all, the Holy Spirit to energize us to hold onto the greater promises of God.

I was presenting some seminars on the struggle with porn at the Keswick Convention in the Lake District in the United Kingdom. During a break I climbed the mountain Skiddaw with a friend, approaching the summit from the steeper west side. It was hard work! The final push is across loose rock at a forty-five-degree angle. Each step is agony. The calves are aching as you try to lift your weight on tired legs. It feels like a form of torture—and this is what we do for leisure! So why do we do it? Why don't we just give up? Because we're confident that the view from the top will make all the effort seem worthwhile. And so it was, for me and my friend.

This is a great picture of the way we're sanctified by faith. Sometimes it can be agony. Each step is hard work. You feel like giving up. But you press on, because faith tells you that the view from the top will be glorious. Legalism would make you climb the slope by berating you or beating you down. And if you've ever tried climbing a mountain with reluctant children, you'll know that that approach doesn't work very well. At best you might get them up one mountain, but you'll not get them up a second! The gospel gets you up the mountain by promising you a glorious view from the top. The path is no less hard, but there's a spring in your step as you anticipate what's coming. Faith is fixing your eyes on the mountain top. Every now and then you can turn round and get a glimpse of the glorious view, just as we experience more of God the more we know him and serve him. And those glimpses are a foretaste of what's to come: the mountain top of God's eternal glory.

PORN AS SELF-WORSHIP

The false promises of porn are the sin behind the sin of porn. But there's one more layer to unravel. There's something that lurks even behind the lies of porn. Underlying all these false promises is the desire to be worshiped. One of the participants in my research described porn as "a worship disorder."

One of the common characteristics of porn is that women readily express pleasure. "I like to see the pleasure and ecstasy on her face as she lets herself go," says Karl. Even in softcore porn, the woman looks into the camera with "come-on" eyes. The very act of posing is designed to communicate that she is there for *you*. "Porn is a lie," says

Geoff. "It teaches a man that he is desired by the most beautiful woman on earth."

At the heart of porn is self-worship. Here is a world in which people worship me. I project myself onto the stud in the film and imagine women crying out to me in adoration. I'm worshiped for my potency and power. Jack says, "I guess I dream of being some sort of stud that can make all women happy."

When you view porn, you can move from image to image, and each woman is there for you, offering herself to you. They all want you, and you can choose between them. Not only are you adored, but you have sovereign power. "Porn gives me power," acknowledges Tyrone. "I can choose the body of my sexual 'partner.' I can find porn in which they will do anything I can think of. It's really the worship of myself, trying to convince myself I'm powerful and irresistible." Carl Trueman comments:

> In its virtual elimination of the body, the computer world offers users the potential (albeit illusory) of transcending their bodily limitations. On Facebook, I can be anybody I want to be: an eighteen year old Californian with a six-pack, good teeth, a sun tan and a pilot's license; or even a 25 year old blonde beauty queen from North Carolina with a degree in astrophysics. I can become the ultimate in self-created beings. . . . In virtual world . . . I can be anyone I choose to be. I am the Creator; or at least, I have the potential to think I am.[19]

Or consider an explanation from another porn user: "I use porn because my spouse doesn't have a rampant desire to fulfill needs." Why isn't it enough for our spouse to be willing to have sex with us? That would be enough to celebrate and reinforce our love. But, no, that's not enough. She must have a "rampant desire." Why? Because what I long for is to be worshiped. I want my sexual partner to simper before me, overcome with desire, under my sexual power. But I'm not a sex god, and my wife just wants ordinary sex. In fact, she may just want a cuddle. But that's not enough—I demand to be worshiped.

And so I turn instead to porn, because in porn every woman I see worships me.

Porn promises big time but fails to deliver every time. It promises intimacy comfort, relief. It delivers loneliness, pain, guilt. I suppose I worship myself. It's getting what I want, when I want it, how I want it. I'm in control. So I turn to porn instead of God because it means I can remain proud, I can remain in control, I don't have to humble myself.

REPENTANCE: TURNING FROM SELF TO WORSHIP GOD

We become Christians through faith and repentance. We continue and grow by ongoing faith and repentance. And this means that we counter porn through faith and repentance. Battling porn with faith means embracing the truth about God in place of the false promises of porn. Battling porn with repentance means turning from self to worship God.

When tempted to use porn, remind yourself that it's a temptation to self-worship. We need a fundamental shift of orientation. We need to move from acting as if "It's all about me" to acting as if "It's all about you, Lord."

This begins with adoration. Our second ingredient in the battle against porn is *an adoration of God—a desire for God arising from a confidence that he offers more than porn.* Instead of self-worship, we must worship God. Consider his merits, his worth, his glory, his beauty, his kindness, his grace, his majesty, his holiness, his power. So who will you worship today?

Call yourself away from yourself—from selfishness—to self-denial and service. With every false promise of porn there is not only a gospel promise, but a corresponding gospel virtue. Call yourself to action: to commitment, to responsibility, to service, to patience, to humility, to glory. There is joy to be found in doing the right thing. It's time to be a man (if you are a man!). We've seen that porn offers potency. It makes us feel manly. But here's where we can be *truly* manly—when we take responsibility, when we battle, when we find comrades to fight with us.

Table 3. Turning from the Promises of Porn to the Adoration of God

Promise of Porn	Typical Context	Faith in God	Gospel Virtue
respect	inadequacy and fear of rejection	God is glorious—he is the one we should fear	Call yourself to pursue God's glory
relationship	fear of intimacy and risk	God is great—he is sovereign over our relationships	Call yourself to commitment
refuge	hardship and fear of failure	God is great—he is sovereign over our lives	Call yourself to responsibility
reward	boredom and sacrifice	God is good—he is our ultimate and lasting joy	Call yourself to service
revenge	frustration and anger	God is gracious—he gives us more than we deserve	Call yourself to patience
redemption	guilt and self-loathing	God is gracious—he is the one who atones for our sin	Call yourself to humility

DIAGNOSIS

The diagnostic chart in table 3 summarizes what we've seen. Not all of it will apply to you. It's designed to help you identify the roots of your porn habit. Where are you on this chart? What remedy does it suggest for your porn habit?

FIGHTING PLEASURE WITH GREATER PLEASURE

Porn is a sin of the imagination. We need to counter it by enlarging our imaginations. The answer to porn is to believe the truth. But that's so much more than an intellectual process. We need to let the truth capture our imaginations: to meditate, ponder, wonder at and sing the truth. We need to feel the truth, glory in the truth, delight in the truth. Discipline yourself to start each day by cultivating your affections for God. Remind yourself of Christ's goodness, glory, grace and greatness until your heart is warmed again by those truths and Christ is supreme in your heart. "Guard your heart above all else, for it determines the course of your life" (Proverbs 4:23 NLT).

One Christian who's struggled with porn concludes:

> Modern conservative evangelicalism fuels sex addiction because it has come to focus on the externals of religion, not the affections. By externals I mean such things as confessions, dogmas, personal priorities, church growth strategies, church attendance, training courses, evangelism, Bible study groups and so on: things that are visible in a believer's life. By affections, I mean those things that cannot be heard or seen directly—fears, loves, joys, delights, hates, anxieties: the currents that swirl in the waters of a believer's heart; the hidden desires that lie deep beneath our decisions. . . . If we are going to help people struggling with sex addiction, we need to recognize that the manger in which their sin is cradled is not the intellect, but the heart, the seat of their desires. They therefore need something more than mere information: they need to be wooed by the true and pure lover that their heart secretly seeks.[20]

Jesus offers living water. Battling porn in our lives is not an exercise in denying pleasure. It's about fighting pleasure with greater pleasure.

> The fire of lust's pleasures must be fought with the fire of God's pleasures. If we try to fight the fire of lust with prohibitions and threats alone—even the terrible warnings of Jesus—we will fail. We must fight it with a massive promise of superior happiness. We must swallow up the little flicker of lust's pleasure in the conflagration of holy satisfaction.[21]

We don't need to say to ourselves, "I should not use porn." The good news is that we can say to ourselves, "I don't *need* to use porn, because God is bigger and better."

3

Freed by the Grace of God

CAN YOU RELATE TO ANY OF THESE statements from porn users? "I feel crap about myself. I don't feel worthy to serve God. And I don't believe I can break the habit." "It's made me want to hide from God. I've seen him as a severe judge, displeased with me. It makes me doubt my salvation, and then the depression comes and with the depression comes temptation to sin again." "I wrestle with what it means to repent and be forgiven, given the repetitious nature of the problem. I feel caught between taking God's grace for granted and forever carrying the guilt with me, as though my repentance isn't enough."

FALSE HOPE: SELF-RIGHTEOUSNESS

Here are three common reasons why people want to kick their porn habit:

- to prove ourselves to God—so he will bless us or save us
- to prove ourselves to other people—so people like us or approve of us
- to prove ourselves to ourselves—so we feel good about ourselves

But we can't prove ourselves. We can't justify ourselves before God. "There is no one righteous," says the Bible, "not even one"; "all have sinned and fall short of the glory of God" (Romans 3:10, 23).

None of these reasons work, because they put "me" at the center of my change project. And putting yourself at the center is pretty much a definition of sin! "Pornography was a sin," says Felix, "but so too was the self-justifying reaction of my flesh that wanted to hide from it and work my way back into God's graces." Patrick says, "My view of God had become extremely limited. I couldn't talk with him about my problems. My picture of him was that he would only accept me if and when I 'scrubbed up' enough."

Jesus told a story of two people going to pray in the temple:

> To some who were confident of their own righteousness and looked down on everybody else, Jesus told this parable: "Two men went up to the temple to pray, one a Pharisee and the other a tax collector. The Pharisee stood up and prayed about himself: 'God, I thank you that I am not like other men—robbers, evildoers, adulterers—or even like this tax collector. I fast twice a week and give a tenth of all I get.'
>
> "But the tax collector stood at a distance. He would not even look up to heaven, but beat his breast and said, 'God, have mercy on me, a sinner.'
>
> "I tell you that this man, rather than the other, went home justified before God. For everyone who exalts himself will be humbled, and he who humbles himself will be exalted." (Luke 18:9-14)

The Pharisees were a zealous religious sect within Judaism. This Pharisee thought his good works could make him right with God. So his "prayer" is really a public boast. It's all about him. "I am not like other men. . . . I fast. . . . I give." Jesus told this parable to people "who were confident of their own righteousness." Like the Pharisee in the story, they thought they were OK with God because of what they did. But they were in for a shock. Jesus says it's not enough. No one can make up for the sin they've committed. In fact, our righteousness actually makes things worse. Sin is more than doing bad things; it is a state of rebellion. It's a rejection of God and his good rule. Self-righteousness is simply another form of that rebellion. It's another way of saying, "I can manage in life without God." Our proud self-righteousness only gets in the way. It stops us turning to God for mercy, because instead we vainly opt to manage on our own.

TRUE HOPE: THE MERCY OF GOD

The other man in the story is a tax collector. Tax collectors were collaborators with the Roman occupiers, so everyone despised them as traitors. Indeed, not only were they traitors against the nation, but they were on the side of God's enemies. There was surely no way a tax collector could be right with God! Can an enemy of God become his friend? Yet Jesus says the tax collector went home "justified." What makes the tax collector right with God is not his righteousness but God's mercy. What he "does" in the story is cry out to God for mercy: "God, have mercy on me, a sinner."

Some people understand this in their heads, but the assault of pornography makes it hard to feel it as a reality for them:

> I feel dirty and unable to approach God after looking at porn. I feel hypocritical when seeking God's blessings or doing work for him. I know from experience as well as Scripture that he'll forgive me, time and time again. But so often I feel unable to come to him in repentance, even though I know my sin is already dealt with.

> It's made me feel like not approaching God for a while. I know my justified status before God doesn't change, but it's difficult to be in touch with that truth experientially if you find yourself continually indulging in things you know he hates.

Yet Jesus *lived* God's welcome to sinners. He embodied God's mercy. He was known as the friend of sinners (Luke 7:34). The religious people didn't like it, because it turned their proud systems of self-righteousness upside down (Luke 5:27-30; 15:1-2). But Jesus sat down to eat with prostitutes, adulterers and porn addicts.

TRUE HOPE: THE CROSS OF CHRIST

Jesus not only lived God's welcome to sinners, he died to make God's welcome to sinners possible. The problem with trying to prove ourselves is not simply that it doesn't work but that it's a denial of Christ's saving work. In Romans 8:3-4 Paul says:

> For what the law was powerless to do in that it was weakened by the sinful nature, God did by sending his own Son in the likeness of sinful man to be a sin offering. And so he condemned sin in sinful man, in order that the righteous requirements of the law might be fully met in us, who do not live according to the sinful nature but according to the Spirit.

Let me make explicit what this means for porn users:

> For what the law was powerless to do in that it was weakened by the sinful nature, God did by sending his own Son in the likeness of porn users to be an offering for the sin of porn. And so he condemned the sin of porn in sinful man, in order that the requirements of sexual purity might be fully met in us, who do not live according to the sinful nature but according to the Spirit.

On the cross, God treated Christ as a porn user. He condemned the sin of porn users in Christ. And Christ cried, "It is finished." In 2 Corinthians 5:21 Paul says, "God made him who had no sin to be sin for us, so that in him we might become the righteousness of God." Again, let's be clear what this means for Christians who struggle with porn: "God made Jesus, who never looked with lust, to be a porn addict for us, so that in him we might become sexually pure." Amazing! "Therefore, there is now no condemnation for those who are in Christ Jesus" (Romans 8:1).

YOU ARE SEXUALLY PURE

So you're sexually pure in God's sight. When God looks at you he doesn't see "a sad wanker." He sees the righteousness of Christ. "Christ loved the church and gave himself up for her make her holy, cleansing her by the washing with water through the word," says Paul. And so God now sees us as "a radiant church, without stain or wrinkle or any other blemish, but holy and blameless" (Ephesians 5:25-27).

Wake up, wake up, O Zion!
Clothe yourself with strength.
Put on your beautiful clothes, O holy city of Jerusalem,
for unclean and godless people will enter your gates no longer.
Rise from the dust, O Jerusalem.
Sit in a place of honor.
Remove the chains of slavery from your neck,
O captive daughter of Zion.
For this is what the LORD says:
"When I sold you into exile,
I received no payment.
Now I can redeem you
without having to pay for you." (Isaiah 52:1-3 NLT)

God's people have been defiled (the unclean have entered them) and dishonored (they are in the dust). And people who are treated as nothing may often think of themselves as nothing. They may think they're "damaged goods" or "dirty people." But the Lord challenges his people to see themselves as he sees them. We're dressed in beautiful clothes—literally "garments of splendor"—and seated in places of honor. We've been redeemed with the precious blood of Jesus. You've been redeemed, cleansed and clothed. Your spouse with a sinful past has been redeemed, cleansed and clothed. Listen to Roger's testimony:

> I struggled with doubting my salvation a lot whenever I was at the height of my addiction. I felt I'd committed sins that couldn't be forgiven. Or, later, I'd embrace forgiveness, but not believe I could change. So I thought I was condemned to a limping, hamstrung relationship with God. Seeing God deliver me, in large measure, from the condemnation and the addiction of pornography has been one of the key ways I've learned the power and scope of his grace in Christ.

HIDING FROM THE HELP WE NEED

Recognizing our acceptance by God is crucial in overcoming porn. So here's our third key ingredient in the battle against porn: *an acceptance of grace—an assurance that you are right with God and loved by God through faith in the work of Jesus.*

Table 4. Third Key Ingredient in the Battle Against Porn

1	abhorence of porn	a hatred of porn itself (not just the shame it brings) and a longing for change
2	adoration of God	a desire for God, arising from a confidence that he offers more than porn
3	assurance of grace	an assurance that you are loved by God and right with God through faith in the work of Jesus
4	avoidance of temptation	a commitment to do all in your power to avoid temptation, starting with controls on your computer
5	accountability to others	a community of Christians who are holding you accountable and supporting you in your struggle

Here's why this is so important. You can't change your porn habit on your own. You need God's help, his forgiveness, his freedom and his transforming power. You need the promises of his Word and the energy of his Spirit.

But you won't come to God if you feel unworthy to do so. "Porn's presence in my life," says Peter, "often made me feel guilty and unworthy to come before God in prayer." "It takes me away from the cross," says Ian, "I feel dirty, so I don't want to come to Jesus in prayer and ask for forgiveness." Frank says, "Lust turns us inward toward ourselves and not outward toward our spouse, or toward God. 'Adam, where are you?' 'Full of shame and hiding, Lord!' " Frank hits upon something important. A porn user can feel like Adam in the garden after he rejected God (Genesis 3:8): naked, exposed, ashamed and hiding from God. We desperately need God, but we're hiding from him.

But God is like the father in the parable of the prodigal son. He's looking for you and is ready to run to meet you, to throw his arms around you and embrace you in his love. God isn't frowning on you; he is smiling at you as a father. God says to us, "Look to the cross. See there my love. See there my provision. All your sin is dealt with. You're right with me. You're clothed in Christ. Your righteousness isn't enough; it's never enough. But Christ's righteousness covers every-thing. In Christ you're worthy. In Christ you're beautiful. In Christ you're pure. You are washed, cleansed, sanctified. Come to me!"

"Therefore, since we have been justified through faith, we have peace with God through our Lord Jesus Christ, through whom we have gained access by faith into this grace in which we now stand" (Romans 5:1-2). Porn users are God's enemies. There's absolutely no doubt about that. But through his death, Christ has made peace be-tween us and God. We're now right with God through faith. Peace has been declared, and so we can access the grace of God.

To break your porn habit, you'll need to receive mercy and find grace from God to help you in your time of need. I have good news for you:

> Since we have a great high priest who has gone through the heavens, Jesus the Son of God, let us hold firmly to the faith we profess. For we do not have a high priest who is unable to sym-pathize with our weaknesses, but we have one who has been tempted in every way, just as we are—yet was without sin. Let us then approach the throne of grace with confidence, so that we may receive mercy and find grace to help us in our time of need. (Hebrews 4:14-16)

Greg comments, "You can't overcome it alone. God still loves you. Christ still died for you. Jesus was tempted in every way—yet was without sin. He understands the pressure of temptation. We don't draw near to an uncaring, unsympathetic Savior." Christ died so that you can "draw near to God with a sincere heart in full assurance of faith, having our hearts sprinkled to cleanse us from a guilty conscience and having our bodies washed with pure water" (Hebrews 10:22). To win the battle against porn, you need to keep drawing near to God, and that movement starts with confidence in his gracious welcome.

THE FIRST STEP OUT OF PORN IS A STEP DOWN

The main reason we don't change is our proud self-righteousness and our proud self-reliance. Porn and pride go hand in hand. It's an odd dynamic, because porn brings so much shame. But we've seen that porn also puts me at the center, creating a world in which I'm worshiped. So despite the shame it brings, it strongly reinforces our pride.

In our proud self-righteousness we excuse sin or minimize it or hide it. "I occasionally slip up," we tell ourselves, "but it's not a big problem." "It's tough for me at the moment—that's why I do it." Or we recognize the problem, but we don't want anyone else to find out. We don't want other people to see us as someone with a porn problem.

In our proud self-reliance we think we can beat it on our own. Jesus begins the Sermon on the Mount with these words: "Blessed are the poor in spirit, for theirs is the kingdom of heaven" (Matthew 5:3). "Blessed are the broken people," we might say, or "Blessed are the desperate people."

I met regularly with Gordon. "I really disappoint myself when I slip up and look at porn," he would say to me. I began to realize that, for Gordon, porn was primarily a sin against himself. It ruined his self-image. It stopped him being a man everyone could admire. The problem was that porn fed that pride, creating an alternative world in which he was admired.

So change must begin with humility and brokenness. The first step out of porn is a step down. We need to begin by humbling ourselves. We need to give up our self-righteousness and our self-reliance and look instead to the righteousness of Christ. We need to stop waiting until we're worthy of God and in humility receive his grace.

He gives us more grace. That is why Scripture says:
"God opposes the proud
but gives grace to the humble."

Submit yourselves, then, to God. Resist the devil, and he will flee from you. Come near to God and he will come near to you.

Wash your hands, you sinners, and purify your hearts, you double-minded. Grieve, mourn and wail. Change your laughter to mourning and your joy to gloom. Humble yourselves before the Lord, and he will lift you up. (James 4:6-10)

QUALIFIED FOR SERVICE, FIT FOR ACTION

"How can I, such a continual and obvious sinner, hope to be of service to Jesus?" "When I fail in this area, I feel unworthy and generally lacking any motivation to serve Christ. I wonder whether my struggle should disqualify me from ministry, but I'm too ashamed to ask anybody for help because I'm in a new church and I worry too much what people think of me."

Continued use of porn will make it hard for you to serve God well. Your service will be characterized by joyless duty and complaint because you're not finding joy in Christ but looking for it elsewhere. Your ability to proclaim the goodness of God will be compromised because you don't find him good enough for you. You'll find it hard to view Christian women as sisters because you're used to viewing women as objects. You'll find it hard to confront Christian brothers for fear they might challenge you in return.

But using porn doesn't disqualify you from serving God. For one thing, you were never qualified in the first place! God didn't call you to his service because you were a great and godly person. Second, God uses broken people. Noah was a drunkard. Jacob was a cheat. Moses was a murderer. Gideon was a coward. David was an adulterer. Jeremiah was a depressive. Matthew was a traitor. James and John were hotheads. Simon the Zealot was a terrorist. Peter was all talk. Paul was a persecutor of God's people. And then there's Samson. Every act of deliverance that Samson undertook started with his uncontrolled lust (Judges 14:1-4; 15:1-3; 16:1-3, 4). Yet there he is, among the heroes of the faith in Hebrews 11:32. Third, God qualifies for his service by the redemption of Christ and the power of the Spirit. Your porn may be a big problem, but it's not bigger than Jesus or the Spirit.

So there are two requirements for serving God. First, you must be committed to struggling with porn. Those who don't see porn as an issue are disqualified. You don't have to be fixed—if you did, then no one would be qualified to lead God's people. But you do have to be facing in the right direction, desiring God and holiness.

Second, you must rely on God's grace. George came to tell me he'd visited sex chatrooms. "I guess this mean I'll have to step down as a leader," he said toward the end of our conversation. "It depends on whether you really believe in justification by faith," I replied. It's no use pretending the problem is small or insignificant—porn will wreak havoc in your ministry. But the make-or-break issue is whether you look to Christ for your righteousness.

If you don't feel worthy in Christ, or you look to yourself for your worth, then you shouldn't lead God's people. Your leadership will be joyless, complaining and oppressive. You'll hide, rather than being vulnerable. You'll fear exposure. You'll minimize sin. You'll condemn others to boost your own self-image. The fruit of your ministry will be other legalists. What disqualifies us for service is not the use of porn but a lack of faith in the completed work of Christ.

But if you do trust in Christ, you will be—as you always were—one sinner pointing other sinners to the source of grace, one hungry beggar telling other hungry beggars about the bread of life.

GUTSY GUILT

In 2007 John Piper wrote an article in *Christianity Today* called "Gutsy Guilt." In it he describes speaking at a conference with George Verwer, the founder of Operation Mobilization:

> Verwer's burden at that conference was the tragic number of young people who at one point in their lives dreamed of radical obedience to Jesus, but then faded away into useless American prosperity. A gnawing sense of guilt and unworthiness over sexual failure gradually gave way to spiritual powerlessness and the dead-end dream of middle-class security and comfort.[1]

Many young people, argues Piper, are not getting involved in mission because they don't know how to deal with sexual failure. The tragedy is not masturbation and pornography. "The tragedy is that Satan uses guilt from these failures to strip you of every radical dream you ever had or might have. In their place, he gives you a happy, safe, secure, American life of superficial pleasures, until you die in your lakeside rocking chair."

The "gutsy guilt" that Piper calls us to is the attitude of those who are guilty but don't let Satan use that guilt to destroy their service of God. They have the guts to take on Satan, to counter his accusations with faith in the finished work of Christ.

People like Henry need "gutsy guilt." He wrote, "The struggle took over my life completely. I found it very difficult to continue in my relationship with God and in my service for him. . . . I still continued to serve God, but constantly Satan reminded me of my sinful state and this caused a stumbling block in my faith."

Paul says that Christ "disarmed" Satan by nailing the record of our sin to the cross (Colossians 2:14-15). Satan says to us, "How can you serve God after all you've done?" And in and of ourselves we have no response, because it's true: we aren't worthy to serve God. But in Christ we can reply, "Yes, I am an unworthy sinner, but Christ has taken the record of my sin and nailed it the cross. So get out of my way! I'm off to serve God and his people." Piper concludes with these words:

> When you learn to deal with the guilt of sexual failure by this kind of broken-hearted boldness, this kind of theology, this kind of justification by faith, this kind of substitutionary atonement, this kind of gutsy guilt, you will fall less often. Why is this so? Because Christ will become increasingly precious to you.
>
> Best of all, Satan will not be able to destroy your dream of a life of radical obedience to Christ. By this Christ-exalting gutsy guilt, thousands of you will give your lives to spread a passion for the supremacy of God in all things for the joy of all peoples through Jesus Christ.

CLEAN TO BE CLEAN

So why change? If not to earn approval or to qualify for service, then why change?

We change so that, more and more, we live out our new identity in Christ. The commands (imperatives) of the gospel are always rooted in its descriptions of who we are in Christ (the indicatives). We're called to be what we are in Christ.

In living our new identity we embrace a life of freedom, love, hope and joy. The call to holiness in the New Testament is not a call to duty, drudgery, repression and boredom, but always a call to joy, meaning, satisfaction and fulfilment. Our problem too often is that we lack the faith to see this. Porn seems like a better option. We fail to look beyond the moment and see the joy that God offers us in Christ.

In 1 Corinthians 6 Paul addresses Christians involved in sexual immorality. He is clear that God condemns sexually immoral behavior. No one who is sexually immoral will enter God's kingdom, he tells the Corinthians (vv. 9-10). But he doesn't then tell the Corinthians to reform their behavior or face that fate. No. He says, "And that is what some of you were. But you were washed, you were sanctified, you were justified in the name of the Lord Jesus Christ and by the Spirit of our God" (1 Corinthians 6:11). He doesn't tell the Corinthians what to do, but who they are and what God has done for them. They are clean, holy, righteous in God's sight. How is that a motive for change?

Free to be free. First, God has set us free to be free. " 'Everything is permissible for me'—but not everything is beneficial. 'Everything is permissible for me'—but I will not be mastered by anything" (1 Corinthians 6:12). "Everything is permissible for me" is almost certainly a Corinthian slogan. "We're free—we're not bound by law anymore." Yes, says Paul, but God set you free to be free—not to be mastered by sin all over again. That's not freedom. That's like a captive, released after years in solitary confinement, saying, "I'm going to use my freedom to live in a dirty prison cell."

Clean to be clean. Second, God has washed us (1 Corinthians 6:11) so we can be clean. "'Food for the stomach and the stomach for food'—but God will destroy them both. The body is not meant for sexual immorality, but for the Lord, and the Lord for the body. By his power God raised the Lord from the dead, and he will raise us also" (1 Corinthians 6:13-14). "Food for the stomach and the stomach for food" is probably another Corinthian slogan. It was a way of saying that what happens with our bodies doesn't really matter. "Our bodies are just eating machines," the Corinthians said. "They're not the real us. Sleeping with prostitutes is no big deal because it only involves our physical bodies; it doesn't involve our souls."

Paul's counterslogan is "the body for the Lord, and the Lord for the body." Body and soul can't be so easily divided. Christ gave his body to save our bodies, and one day God will raise our bodies with Christ. The body is not expendable. It's part of God's salvation. And so we give our bodies to the One who gave his body for us. God saved our bodies so they can be used for his glory. He washed our bodies so they can be clean.

Imagine working on your car all day. And then you come in and get scrubbed up, ready for a meal out with your wife. You take a shower, scrub your hands, shave and iron a newly washed shirt. And then, while you are waiting for your wife, you think, *I'll just spend ten minutes more on that job.* And ten minutes later, you and your clothes are covered in grease all over again. That's what using porn is like when you've been washed by the Holy Spirit. "Do not offer the parts of your body to sin, as instruments of wickedness, but rather offer yourselves to God, as those who have been brought from death to life; and offer the parts of your body to him as instruments of righteousness" (Romans 6:13).

United to be united. Third, God has united us with Christ in his resurrection so we can enjoy union with Christ. As Gordon Cheng acknowledges, if we had been in Paul's situation we might have written something like this: "Now, about prostitutes: stop visiting them. And while you're about it, stop downloading porn onto your hard drive. . . . Here's a link to a downloadable anti-pornography program that will help. Now get on with living the right way!"[2]

There's no doubt that Paul disapproves of visiting prostitutes. But this isn't the approach he takes. Instead, he talks about the resurrection:

> By his power God raised the Lord from the dead, and he will raise us also. Do you not know that your bodies are members of Christ himself? Shall I then take the members of Christ and unite them with a prostitute? Never! Do you not know that he who unites himself with a prostitute is one with her in body? For it is said, "The two will become one flesh." But he who unites himself with the Lord is one with him in spirit. (1 Corinthians 6:14-17)

Again Paul tells the Corinthians who they are: people united with Christ in his resurrection. Should a member of Christ be united with a prostitute? Of course not! We've been united with Christ so that we can enjoy union with Christ. It's in Christ that true joy is found. And one day your body—the very body you inhabit now, the very body you use for pornography—will be raised by God for union with Christ.

Holy to be holy. Fourth, God has sanctified us or made us holy by the Holy Spirit (1 Corinthians 6:11) so we can be a home for the Holy Spirit of God: "Flee from sexual immorality. All other sins a man commits are outside his body, but he who sins sexually sins against his own body. Do you not know that your body is a temple of the Holy Spirit, who is in you, whom you have received from God?" (1 Corinthians 6:18-19).

The temple was the sign of God's holy presence among his people, a beautiful and glorious symbol, but also awesome and terrible. Only the priests could enter the holy place, and only the high priest could enter the holy of holies, the place where the ark of the covenant was located, and then only once a year through a blood sacrifice (Hebrews 9:1-10). The temple and its sacrifices were a pointer to Jesus (Hebrews 9:11-28). He is God with us, and through his blood we come into God's presence.

All that the temple represented is now a reality in your life. God's glorious, holy, awesome, terrifying presence is in you, through the Holy Spirit. So sleeping with a prostitute or using porn is an act of defilement, like committing an act of defilement in the holy of holies. I hardly dare write it, but this is the force of Paul's argument: it's like having sex with a prostitute on the ark of the covenant. Such an act is unthinkable.

Valued to be valuable. Fifth, God has bought you with the price of his own Son: "You are not your own; you were bought at a price. Therefore honor God with your body" (1 Corinthians 6:19-20). You belong to him. You're not free to give yourself away to anyone or anything else. You may not have been a thing of value, but now you are. We're not valued by God because we're inherently valuable. It's the other way round. We're valuable because we are valued by God, and the value he places on us is the precious blood of Jesus. Time and again, people engage in sexual sin because they think they're worthless. So they seek affirmation in sex, or they think they're not worth keeping pure. But whatever your past, God has now given you worth. You're worth the price of his own Son. You belong to him. Honor God with your body.

THE FEAST OF PORN AND THE FEAST OF GOD

So let's sum up our motive for change: *to enjoy the freedom from porn and delight in God that God gives to us through Jesus.*[3] I want to highlight four things from this definition.

First, growing in holiness is about joy, discovering true joy—the joy of knowing and serving God. There is self-denial—sometimes hard and painful self-denial—but true self-denial leads to gaining your life (Mark 8:34-37). There will be times when we act out of duty, but we do this believing that duty leads to joy and denying yourself leads to gaining your life.

Second, change is about living in freedom. We refuse to go back to the chains and filth of our porn. We live in the wonderful freedom that God has given us. We're released to be the people we should be.

Third, change is about discovering the delight of knowing and serving God. Our job is to stop grubbing around in the dirt and instead to enjoy knowing God. We give up our cheap imitations and enjoy the real thing. Holiness is recognizing that the pleasures of porn are empty and temporary, while God is inviting us to magnificent, true, full and rich pleasures that last forever.

Fourth, becoming like Jesus is something that God gives to us, not an achievement that we offer to God. It's enjoying the new identity he's given us in Christ. He's set us free from sin and offers a relationship with himself.

It's as if there are two feasts: the feast of God and the feast of porn. We're invited to both. God invites us to find satisfaction in him. Sin entices us with its lies to look for satisfaction in porn. So we're double-booked. All the time, we have to choose which feast we attend. This is God's invitation to us:

> Come, all you who are thirsty,
>   come to the waters;
> and you who have no money,
>   come, buy and eat!
> Come, buy wine and milk
>   without money and without cost.
> Why spend money on what is not bread,
>   and your labor on what does not satisfy?
> Listen, listen to me, and eat what is good,
>   and your soul will delight in the richest of fare. (Isaiah 55:1-2)

Porn promises so much, but it doesn't satisfy and charges a high price: broken lives, broken relationships, broken hopes. Ultimately, the wages of porn is death. But God offers us a feast that satisfies, a delight for our souls. The motivation for change and holiness is this: God's feast is so much better! And the price tag reads, "No cost." It's his gift. So whose feast are you going to attend today?

FREED BY THE POWER OF GOD

You may have tried and failed to change in the past. But there is hope, because God is in the business of change. God creates in us a new heart with new desires. Other therapies can modify behavior. But only God can bring true and lasting change, liberating us from the slavery of porn.

God the Father uses all the circumstances of our lives to shape our hearts and conform our lives into the image of his Son (John 15:1-4; Romans 8:28-30; Hebrews 11:5-11). God the Son sets us free both from the penalty of sin (= death) and from the power of sin (= slavery) (Romans 6:5-6). Our "old self," which lived under the mastery of sin, has died with Christ, and so now we have a new self under the mastery of God. God the Spirit gives us the power to live the new life that Jesus gives and new desires for God and for holiness (John 3:3-8; Galatians 5:16-25). The Father sanctifies through the Son by the Spirit.

"Don't content yourself with external means like Internet filters, commitments not to bring your computer up to your room, and accountability," says Kyle. "Let the gospel sink in deep and do its work on your heart about pornography. The solution is Christ crucified and resurrected, not just a commitment on your part."

> It is for freedom that Christ has set us free. Stand firm, then, and do not let yourselves be burdened again by a yoke of slavery. . . .
>
> You, my brothers, were called to be free. But do not use your freedom to indulge the sinful nature; rather, serve one another in love. . . .
>
> So I say, live by the Spirit, and you will not gratify the desires of the sinful nature. For the sinful nature desires what is contrary to the Spirit, and the Spirit what is contrary to the sinful nature. They are in conflict with each other, so that you do not do what you want. . . .
>
> The acts of the sinful nature are obvious: sexual immorality, impurity and debauchery. . . .
>
> But the fruit of the Spirit is love, joy, peace, patience, kindness, goodness, faithfulness, gentleness and self-control.

Against such things there is no law. Those who belong to Christ Jesus have crucified the sinful nature with its passions and desires. Since we live by the Spirit, let us keep in step with the Spirit. (Galatians 5:1, 13, 16-17, 19, 22-25)

Christ sets us free for freedom, not for ongoing slavery to our sinful natures. And so Christ sends his Spirit into our hearts. The Spirit gives us new desires for holiness. Suddenly battle is joined. The old nature with its desire for porn battles against our Spirit-inspired desires for holiness. Once we were enslaved by our sinful desires. Now we have options. Now we can choose patience, goodness, faithfulness, self-control. We can put to death the sinful nature and its desires. We can walk with the Spirit.

Be assured of this: the Spirit will win this battle. Eventually. One day. In all those who are genuinely God's children the Spirit will triumph. God is not a quitter. The outcome is assured. "We know that when he appears, we shall be like him, for we shall see him as he is" (1 John 3:2).

Hundreds of Christians have been set free from an addiction to porn. Here are a few of them:

> When I first got on the Internet, there was a period of about a year when I went to see what was available and ended up going for sexual satisfaction on an occasional basis, even though by this time I was a pastor. Finally, I knew I had to give this up entirely, and I did so only by the grace of God. I've been porn-free for about eight years, though sometimes the mental images come back.

> I now have more reasons not to look at porn than simply that I shouldn't, and so it's generally under control now. I know Jesus died to free me from stuff like that and his Spirit can help me change.

> I masturbated from the age of ten. But I haven't looked at porn since October 2007, and I haven't masturbated since the same

time. I'd never had a wet dream until December, and it was the weirdest thing ever. I thought at first I was peeing my pants! I knew then that I had turned my back on the addiction.

About ten months ago I managed to stop looking at porn completely, as well as the masturbation that went along with it. God showed me the depths of my sin, and not long after I no longer wanted to use porn. Most of the temptation went after I had experienced the joy of being free from it.

4

The Fight of Faith

Can you relate to any of these experiences?

I usually started with "just looking at a picture." I used to tell myself that would be it. But inevitably I would then end up looking at more hardcore stuff and video clips.

My mind seems to become clouded and tunnelled, and I seem to hunt down satisfaction of my desire to ejaculate.

There's a kind of "wall-breaking" exercise of breaking down one's own defenses bit by bit—looking at something slightly more pornographic each time. So it wouldn't begin by looking at something bad, but build up to it. Strange.

I usually know when I'm going to look at porn long before I actually do. I have plenty of chances to say "no." I just choose to ignore this feeling.

We've seen that change takes place through faith and repentance. We become Christians through faith and repentance, and we grow as Christians through continual faith and repentance.[1] We don't graduate from the gospel to some advanced way of holiness or progress. Martin Luther said, "To progress is always to begin again."[2]

Faith and repentance are not one-off events that take place only when we're converted. John Calvin says, "God assigns to [believers] a race of repentance, which they are to run throughout their lives."[3] By faith we recognize that God offers so much more than the false promises of porn. We fight porn by clinging in faith to the promises of Christ. And we repent of our sinful desire for self-worship and turn instead to worship the living God.

The Bible often uses violent imagery to describe this battle. We're to put to death sinful desires (Romans 8:13; Colossians 3:5). We're to cut off whatever causes us to sin (Matthew 5:27-30). The Bible issues a call to arms. We're to use our bodies as instruments of righteousness (Romans 6:13). We're to fight the good fight of faith (1 Timothy 1:18). We're equipped with spiritual armor for the battle (Ephesians 6:12-18). We battle sinful desires that wage war against our souls (1 Peter 2:11). We're called to be like soldiers on active service (2 Timothy 2:4).

It's time to do battle with porn—to fight the fight of faith. The Bible gives us strategies to reinforce our repentance and strengthen our faith.

KILLING PORN

One way the Bible describes the ongoing activity of repentance is "mortification"—that is, putting sin to death: "Put to death, therefore, whatever belongs to your earthly nature: sexual immorality, impurity, lust, evil desires and greed, which is idolatry" (Colossians 3:5). It means constantly saying a decisive no to sin in our lives, especially at the earliest stages of temptation.

The foundation of mortification is Christ's work on the cross: "For we know that our old self was crucified with [Christ] so that the body of sin might be done away with, that we should no longer be slaves to sin" (Romans 6:6; see also Galatians 2:20; 5:24). It's because we "died with Christ" and "have been raised with Christ" that we're to "put to death . . . whatever belongs to [our] earthly nature" (Colossians 2:20; 3:1, 5). We do this in the power of the Spirit (Romans 8:13). With the Spirit's help, we're active participants in the process of mortification.

We need to get into the habit of saying no the moment tempting thoughts arise. "I think that in the past," concedes Dwayne, "I failed because when temptation came I always flirted with it a little, fooling myself into thinking I could be strong by myself. I didn't flee temptation, and I didn't run to God for help."

The Bible promises: "God is faithful; he will not let you be tempted beyond what you can bear. But when you are tempted, he will also provide a way out so that you can stand up under it" (1 Corinthians 10:13). Sometimes it can seem like we're overpowered by lust. But there's always a way of escape. The problem is that we don't always take that escape route.

We see a woman in the street. We take a second glance. We look at her breasts. We imagine her undressed. We remember a past sexual encounter or porn movie. We play through a sexual fantasy. As we go home, we consider looking at porn on the Internet. *Maybe*, we say to ourselves, *maybe not*, but no firm *no*. *I won't look at porn*, we tell ourselves, *I'll just surf around a bit*—all the time hoping for some titillating material. And then it's *just a quick look*. By now we're hooked. Lust overtakes us. *The temptation was just too strong*, we tell ourselves afterward. But it wasn't at four o'clock, when you first saw the woman in the street. Each step was another opportunity to escape temptation. The way of escape was there all the time; the problem was that we didn't want to take it. There are always many turning points before the point of no return! We need to get into the habit of saying *no* the moment the thought arises.

We also need to get into the habit of not just saying no but saying yes to the glory of God and the beauty of Christ. "The most successful attempts," says Brian, "have always been when I've run to Christ at times of temptation. Singing to God at times of weakness helps me to remember the gospel. I tend not to struggle when I am trusting God and on fire for him at the time—unsurprisingly!"

We need to recognize too that we can view nonpornographic material in a pornographic way. It might be the lingerie section of a clothes catalog or late-night television or undressing a woman on the street with your eyes. It may not technically be porn, but according to Jesus it's adultery (Matthew 5:27-30). And it's a step along the road to explicit porn. A common feature in my questionnaire was men describing how they wouldn't go straight to porn. At first they might dabble around the edges, finding suggestive photos on nonpornographic sites and thinking these would satisfy their desires, when of course they only fed them. So what's the advice of Jesus in these situations?

> You have heard that it was said, "Do not commit adultery." But I tell you that anyone who looks at a woman lustfully has already committed adultery with her in his heart. If your right eye causes you to sin, gouge it out and throw it away. It is better for you to lose one part of your body than for your whole body to be thrown into hell. And if your right hand causes you to sin, cut it off and throw it away. It is better for you to lose one part of your body than for your whole body to go into hell. (Matthew 5:27-30)

Gouge it out. Cut it off. Put it to death. "Be killing sin, or it will be killing you," said the Puritans.

THE MYTH OF SEXUAL RELEASE

There's a popular myth that portrays sexuality as a pressure cooker, a force that grows unless it's expressed. The dangerous thing, we're told, is to suppress or repress that sexual drive. This will either damage a person psychologically or burst out in unhealthy ways. According to this myth, the safest way to release this pressure is either to have sex or to masturbate.

We need to recognize the story that underlies this myth: that we've evolved from animals and retain animal instincts. But the Bible is clear that God set humanity apart from the animals when he made us in his image. We're still, for example, the only animals that wear clothes to cover our nakedness (Genesis 3:7, 21). So we aren't merely animals driven by biological pressures beyond our control.

Instead of the image of the pressure cooker needing periodic release, the Bible speaks of sin as slavery, entanglement and captivity. Sin crouches at our door waiting to control us (Genesis 4:7). The more we indulge our sinful desires, the stronger they become. When we give in to temptation, that temptation goes away, but only for a short time. Lust comes back, sooner and stronger than it did before.

This is why people often binge on porn, using porn repeatedly after long periods of freedom. Rahul says, "I go clean for months at a time, snap, have a binge (three to five times a day for two or three days), and then go clean again." When you've just used porn, those images are in the forefront of your mind. And they don't disappear when you switch off the computer or close the magazine. They linger on into the next day, tempting you to return. Feed temptation and it will return faster and stronger. It's a vicious cycle.

But there's also a virtuous cycle. You can turn from the vicious cycle of porn to the virtuous cycle of freedom. The more you say no to porn, the weaker the temptation will be. Not filling your mind with enticing images means you're less likely to recall them in moments of pressure. Sin is habit-forming, but so too is purity. "Through rejoicing in the gospel at the start of each day," says Ethan, "I'm winning the fight. Temptations come less frequently, and when they come they are weaker—less appealing and less powerful."

BREAKING THE CYCLE OF MASTURBATION

Consider what this means for masturbation. In popular mythology masturbation is the lesser of two evils: it's better to masturbate than find release in extramarital sex.

The Bible doesn't explicitly talk about masturbation. Christians in the past have usually condemned it, but it's become more common in recent years to suggest that it can be legitimate. Perhaps Christians in the past were influenced by negative views of sexuality, but then perhaps today we're influenced by sub-biblical secular psychologies. Because the Bible doesn't address masturbation explicitly, we should be cautious about giving a blanket condemnation. But when you think about masturbating, consider the following.

First, it's a sin to have sex with someone other than your spouse, even if that sex takes place only in your mind. The fact is that masturbation is all but impossible without sexual fantasies, and you need to be confident those fantasies honor God.

Second, masturbation does not relieve sexual tension, except on the most short-term basis. It fuels it. It reinforces sexual thoughts and so usually makes temptation come back sooner and stronger. This is one reason why people think they can't stop masturbating. They get caught in a vicious cycle of desire, which the temporary release of masturbating actually reinforces each time. Every act of ungodly masturbation increases the hold of lust over your life. It's not solving anything. In fact, it's making the problem worse.

Third, masturbation does not involve the self-giving that is integral to sexual intercourse. Masturbation is a self-serving expression of sex outside of the covenant of marriage. There are exceptions to this. The most obvious is mutual masturbation within marriage. Another is when it's part of fertility treatment. But for the most part it's an act of self-love.

At best, then, masturbation is fraught with danger. To use biblical language: "'Everything is permissible for me'—but not everything is beneficial. 'Everything is permissible for me'—but I will not be mastered by anything" (1 Corinthians 6:12).

So ask yourself the following questions:

- Does my masturbation involve inappropriate sexual fantasies?
- Am I in control of my masturbation, or am I being mastered by my masturbation?
- Is my masturbation beneficial? Does it strengthen my marriage? Does it enhance my service of God?
- Is my masturbation something I can do to the glory of God?

The fact that you use porn is a sure-fire sign that your masturbation is ungodly and unhealthy! It is self-evidently out of control and producing harmful fruit in your life.

You may have been masturbating for years. It may have become the normal way you relieve tension, boredom or stress. Life without it seems inconceivable. Its hold on your life seems complete. But I've found that many men can stop habitual masturbation more readily than they imagine. Once they're persuaded that life without masturbation is better than life with masturbation, the virtuous cycle kicks in. Every act of resistance strengthens their resolve for next time. Holiness becomes reinforcing. There are no quick fixes, but habits of thought can be realigned just as habits of action can be.

THE FORTY-DAY CHALLENGE

If either porn or masturbation have become a big or a persistent problem in your life, then I would encourage you to take up the "forty-day challenge." Commit yourself to forty days without any sexual activity—porn, masturbation and sex within marriage. Drs. Mark Laaser and Louis Gregoire say:

> Neuro-chemical tolerance that is a factor in Internet addiction can be reversed if the addict is willing and able to establish a period of total sexual abstinence. This can usually be achieved in 30-90 days, the first 14 of which will be the most difficult. Married [people] should be counselled to negotiate this with his or her spouse. The abstinence period achieves a noticeable detoxification effect. It also begins to reverse a core belief of addicts that sex is their most important need.[4]

AVOIDANCE

The fourth key ingredient in the battle against porn is this: *an avoidance of temptation—a commitment to do all in your power to avoid temptation, starting with controls on your computer.*

Often people begin and end with this ingredient. They think they can defeat porn by putting controls on their computer. But they find it doesn't work. Perhaps they find a way around it, or they find porn elsewhere. Perhaps they find themselves still struggling with past images or sexual fantasies. Avoidance is not enough. We need the other four ingredients. But neither should we despise avoidance. It's an important part of the recipe and a theme throughout the Scriptures.

Table 5. Fourth Key Ingredient in the Battle Against Porn

1	abhorence of porn	a hatred of porn itself (not just the shame it brings) and a longing for change
2	adoration of God	a desire for God, arising from a confidence that he offers more than porn
3	assurance of grace	an assurance that you are loved by God and right with God through faith in the work of Jesus
4	avoidance of temptation	a commitment to do all in your power to avoid temptation, starting with controls on your computer
5	accountability to others	a community of Christians who are holding you accountable and supporting you in your struggle

The Joseph principle—run. "One day [Joseph] went into the house to attend to his duties, and none of the household servants was inside. [His master's wife] caught him by his cloak and said, 'Come to bed with me!' But he left his cloak in her hand and ran out of the house" (Genesis 39:11-12).

The father's wisdom—avoid. "Now then, my sons, listen to me; do not turn aside from what I say. Keep to a path far from [the adulterous woman], do not go near the door of her house" (Proverbs 5:7-8).

The pastor's advice—flee. "Flee from sexual immorality. All other sins a man commits are outside his body, but he who sins sexually sins against his own body" (1 Corinthians 6:18).

Fleeing temptation may not be a complete solution, but it does buy time while we fight the fight of faith. Pete says, "Setting up a Web filter has helped, because I have to undo it if I want to look at something. That gives me an extra hurdle and another minute to think it through. Really, I just need to think about the gospel and that helps enormously."

Here are some well-tried strategies to avoid seeing sexually provocative images:

- Install Internet filter and accountability software, such as Covenant Eyes or XXXchurch.com.
- Give up your movie rental card or let your wife have it.
- Let a Christian friend check your hard drive and mobile.
- Set an appropriate verse or a picture of your family by your screen as a reminder of what matters.
- Manage without Internet access, or access the Internet only through Internet cafés.
- Put Internet access in a public spot in the house.
- Never have a television or computer in the bedroom.
- If your spouse is routinely out one evening of the week, find an activity you can do regularly on that night.
- Have diversion strategies in place—read a good book, watch sports or a movie when you're feeling tempted.
- Go to bed at the same time as other people in the house.
- Don't watch late-night television—put a timer on your television that will switch off at 10:30 p.m.
- Cancel catalogs with lingerie and swimwear sections.
- Avoid shops or locations that create temptation.
- Refuse to participate when colleagues exchange crude jokes or comment on the physical appearance of women.

None of these is a high price to pay—not when eternal glory is at stake. Job said, "I made a covenant with my eyes not to look lustfully at a girl" (Job 31:1).

Accountability software seems to work better than filter software. Filter software blocks porn sites. But people often find ways around this, and if they do then they know they're doing so with impunity. Accountability software informs a partner if you access porn sites.

No doubt there are sites this misses, but you don't know whether this is the case at the time. So your chances of looking at porn without *any* of it registering with your accountability partner are very slim. You can also develop tactics for coping when you face the "triggers" of porn. If you feel a dip after a particular activity (such as the climax of work projects or preaching), then arrange to go to the movies with a friend. If you're going to be alone for a weekend, fill up your time with activity, preferably involving other people. Make sure you get plenty of rest. Kev says, "A key strategy is the avoidance of settings where I would be inclined to view porn: a more balanced work and family schedule keeps stress and boredom to acceptable norms; disciplined Scripture reading, solitude and prayer aid me in recovering balance."

TEN WEAPONS IN THE BATTLE WITH PORN

God has given us "means of grace" to combat porn by reinforcing faith in the promises and glory of God.

1. The Word of God. A lot of phallic language and imagery is about wielding a weapon. This is a key into the way porn works as a substitute for potency, youth and power—a pathetic substitute. The idea that an enemy might quake because someone waggles their willy around is ridiculous. Let's see through porn. Pathetic.

But the Word of God is not pathetic. Here is a mighty sword, the sword of truth. Here is a weapon that can demolish strongholds and cut through pretensions (2 Corinthians 10:4-5). Next time you're tempted to turn to porn to enact potency, turn instead to Ephesians 6. Clothe yourself with the armor of God. "Memorizing Scripture has proved helpful," says Bob. "As I remember and delight in truth, the hollow whispers of falsehood fade away." Wayne says, "In terms of my mental struggles with sexual images and scenarios I find the routine of a daily quiet time, sermons and fellowship to be very helpful. It's a focusing of our eyes on godly things."

Be careful how you relate to Scripture. It's possible to read the Bible, study it, apply correct hermeneutical and exegetical principles, read sound commentaries, explore the meaning of original languages—all with the intent of mastering Scripture or appearing wise. You imagine yourself discoursing on the passage to your home group. It becomes an exercise in pride. Remember the way porn reinforces pride and pride reinforces porn. Regular porn users can study the Bible and come away prouder as a result.

Listen to God.

> This is the one I esteem:
> he who is humble and contrite in spirit,
> and trembles at my word. (Isaiah 66:2)

This is the Bible's central hermeneutic principle—to tremble at God's Word. By all means, study God's Word. But always, always check your heart. Are you reading to master God's Word or to be mastered by it? Does reading God's Word make you proud or does it humble you? Do you search the Scriptures so you can impress others, or do the Scriptures search your heart? Do you tremble as you read?

2. Prayer. Paul concludes his discussion of spiritual armor with these words: "And pray in the Spirit on all occasions with all kinds of prayers and requests. With this in mind, be alert and always keep on praying for all the saints" (Ephesians 6:18). We can't change on our own; we desperately need God's help. Prayer is at the heart of our battle strategy, because the victory is God's. The extent to which you believe this will be reflected in your commitment to prayer. A lack of prayer—or prayer that is just dutiful routine—suggests you think change is really up to you. But if you're desperate for God's help, then you'll cry out to him for mercy. Pray too for people in the sex industry—porn stars and filmmakers. "It's difficult," says Pete, "to enjoy the sins of those you pray for."

3. Fasting. Jesus says those who fast to be seen by people receive their reward in full—the temporary and inconsequential admiration of other people, without the favor of God. But to those who humbly fast, he promises a reward (Matthew 6:16-18). What is this reward? Not a reward that we earn through fasting, as if fasting were some sort of meritorious act. Rather, the reward is God himself. "Blessed are the pure in heart, for they will see God" (Matthew 5:8).

Fasting has a particular role in combating sexual temptation. Hunger and sexual desire are both bodily appetites. Learning to control our appetite for food helps us control our appetite for sex.

There are two dangers associated with fasting. The first is to deny that food is good. Food is a good gift from God and is to be received with enjoyment and thanksgiving (1 Timothy 4:1-5). The second is to think we can earn merit with God through abstinence. Fasting doesn't earn God's approval. The Pharisee who fasts does not go home justified in the parable Jesus tells in Luke 18:12-14, but the sinner who cries out for mercy does. "It's true that we can't win God's approval by what we eat. We don't lose anything if we don't eat it, and we don't gain anything if we do" (1 Corinthians 8:8 NLT).

Since fasting is not in itself meritorious, there is no "right way" to fast. But it's good to stick to whatever you intend. The body suffers from a lack of water long before it suffers from a lack of food, so you should normally continue to drink water during your fast. And don't binge at the end of a long fast.

Think about your sports heroes. Top athletes get up before dawn to train and strictly control their diet. Paul urges us to adopt a spiritual training regime akin to that of athletes:

> Everyone who competes in the games goes into strict training. They do it to get a crown that will not last; but we do it to get a crown that will last forever. Therefore I do not run like a man running aimlessly; I do not fight like a man beating the air. No, I beat my body and make it my slave so that after I have preached to others, I myself will not be disqualified for the prize. (1 Corinthians 9:25-27)

We discipline our bodies so that we control our bodily appetites rather than being controlled by them.

4. Communion. The Lord's Supper is a powerful weapon in the battle against porn. First, it's a reminder of the cross and that we're accepted by God, so that we can draw near to him without fear and find help in the battle. The temple curtain has been torn in two, and we are invited to come to God's table.

Second, it's a kind of enacted feasting on Christ. It's worth considering why Jesus didn't simply give us a form of words to remember the cross: "*Say this* in remembrance of me." The act of eating the bread and drinking the wine is a powerful symbol of finding satisfaction in Christ. It's a reminder that Jesus is the bread of life who gives the satisfaction that porn can never give.

5. Worship. We've seen how porn is a form of self-worship. Every time we worship God we're reminding ourselves that he is bigger and better than anything porn can offer. "One key has been saturating my heart in the gospel and responding in song," says Kyle. "Singing gospel songs has helped me take huge steps in the battle against porn, because gospel songs engage my emotions and my emotions are the place that porn targets."

Paul's condemnation of sexual sin in Ephesians ends with these words: "Speak to one another with psalms, hymns and spiritual songs. Sing and make music in your heart to the Lord, always giving thanks to God the Father for everything, in the name of our Lord Jesus Christ" (Ephesians 5:19-20). Notice that we speak *to one another* in psalms, hymns and spiritual songs. Singing is not simply an act directed to God. It's a call to one another to find delight in God rather than in other things—things like porn.

6. Thanksgiving. Lust says, "I want, I want." Thanksgiving says, "I have, I have. I have so many good things from God." Steve Gallagher says, "Gratitude quenches the fire of lust. A thankful spirit destroys the driving passion for sex because it creates contentment within the man's heart. . . . A grateful heart is a full heart."[5]

Develop some disciplines of gratitude. You may already say a prayer of thanks before meals. Begin or end each day with thanksgiving. Accept gifts and treats with thanksgiving to God. Give thanks before or after sex with your wife: "For everything God created is good, and nothing is to be rejected if it is received with thanksgiving, because it is consecrated by the word of God and prayer" (1 Timothy 4:4-5). Your corrupted sexuality is reconsecrated as you give thanks to God for it.

7. *Community.* We'll talk about accountability partnerships and groups later. But the Christian community offers other ways of helping you avoid porn. Idle time is the devil's playground. So make sure you spend time with other people. Avoid living alone if you can; share a house. And live your life firmly embedded in the wider Christian community. David Powlison says:

> Building real relationships of love with real people is crucial to the transformation of your imagination. You have spent way too much time in your private fantasy world. It's time to build same-sex friendships with people who will hold you accountable and care about you. It's time to build healthy brother-sister relationships with the opposite sex as well. Leave your fictional world of pretend relationships and, if you are a man, start viewing women as your sisters, as people to protect instead of prey upon.[6]

8. *Service.* What was David doing when he saw Bathsheba bathing? The question is rather, what was he *not* doing? It was the time "when kings go off to war" (2 Samuel 11:1). He was neglecting his duty. Service fills our time with diverting activity. More importantly, serving others and taking on responsibility prevents you from being inward in your orientation. Your life stops being "all about me." When Paul tells people not to steal, he also tells them to work hard to give to the poor (Ephesians 4:28). "Stealing involves large amounts of adrenaline," comments Rob Bell.

> What are you channelling your energies into? . . . Life is not about toning down and repressing your God-given life force. It's about channelling it and focusing it and turning it loose on something beautiful, something pure and true and good, something that connects you with God, with others, with the world.[7]

9. Suffering. Suffering is not something we can choose as a means of grace, but it is something we can choose to *interpret* as a means of grace. Peter tells his readers that "all kinds of trials" "have come so that your faith—of greater worth than gold, which perishes even though refined by fire—may be proved genuine and may result in praise, glory and honor when Jesus Christ is revealed" (1 Peter 1:7). Trials in our lives refine our faith. This isn't an automatic process. Suffering can embitter us—we can use it to justify turning to porn. But we can also choose to let suffering refocus our attention on Christ. As some of the good things of this world are stripped away we can choose to find delight in Christ, to say that he is enough.

10. Hope. In his first letter Peter continues: "Though you have not seen [Jesus Christ], you love him; and even though you do not see him now, you believe in him and are filled with an inexpressible and glorious joy, for you are receiving the goal of your faith, the salvation of your souls" (1 Peter 1:8-9). He has already reminded his readers of our "living hope through the resurrection of Jesus Christ from the dead" and our "inheritance that can never perish, spoil or fade—kept in heaven for you" (1 Peter 1:3-4). We don't see Jesus now. Meanwhile, porn is all too visible. But we believe in Jesus, rejoice in hope and look for the day when we will see him. So we're filled with "inexpressible and glorious joy." This is the joy that drives away the desire for porn. We need to cultivate the habit of meditating on the future life. Porn is visible, but its pleasures are temporary. We may not now see Christ, but his glory is eternal.

COMRADES IN THE FIGHT OF FAITH

Rob runs a group for men struggling with porn. "Disclosure is absolutely the first step for people," he told me. "I don't think you can do it by yourself—it's much harder." Steve Gallagher agrees: "If you want to stay stuck in your sin, confess it only to God. If you want to overcome it, confess it to someone else!"[8]

Again and again, people who have overcome pornography testify to the importance of accountability:

It has been a long struggle and, thanks to Christian male friends around my age who've also struggled with it, I've managed to cut the addiction. As with any addiction there are relapses, but now once every few weeks at most.

When I got engaged I confessed to the hold this addiction had on me. Initially my fiancée was crushed and very harsh about it. But the honesty turned out to be very good for accountability, and I've never deliberately accessed Internet pornography since.

"I have weekly accountability and open and honest confession with my roommates," says Jake. "It disarms a lot of the power of shame and guilt when it's brought into the light." This is an allusion to John 3:19-21, when Nicodemus comes to Jesus at night. Jesus says,

> This is the verdict: Light has come into the world, but men loved darkness instead of light because their deeds were evil. Everyone who does evil hates the light, and will not come into the light for fear that his deeds will be exposed. But whoever lives by the truth comes into the light, so that it may be seen plainly that what he has done has been done through God.

Light came into the world in the person of Jesus (John 1:1-9). Jesus is the light (John 8:12), revealing the truth about God. But still, "no one can see the kingdom of God unless he is born again" (John 3:3). Why can't people "see" God's kingdom when Jesus has come into the world? The reason is first that people love the darkness (John 3:19). They don't want to let go of their sin and submit to Jesus. Second, people fear exposure (John 3:20). They don't want to acknowledge their sin and admit their need of a Savior.

Nicodemus comes to Jesus by night because he too fears exposure. He doesn't want to admit his interest in Jesus. Jesus says we're all like that; we don't want to admit our need. We prefer to walk in darkness than be exposed by the light. Nicodemus comes by night and asks, "Why can't I see?" He's a picture of his own question. Underlying all the reasons we give for not knowing God is the fact that we won't admit our need or submit our lives. But the Spirit of God gives new birth (John 3:3, 5) so we can see God's kingdom and live in the light. And "whoever lives by the truth comes into the light, so that it may be seen plainly that what he has done has been done through God" (John 3:21).

A key step is to bring your porn into the light, confessing your sin to someone else, no longer living with the fear of exposure, no longer hiding from God and his people, no longer pretending you can do it on your own.

Our final key ingredient in the battle against porn is this: *accountability to others—a community of Christians who are holding you accountable and supporting you in your struggle.*

Table 6. Fourth Key Ingredient in the Battle Against Porn

1	abhorence of porn	a hatred of porn itself (not just the shame it brings) and a longing for change
2	adoration of God	a desire for God, arising from a confidence that he offers more than porn
3	assurance of grace	an assurance that you are loved by God and right with God through faith in the work of Jesus
4	avoidance of temptation	a commitment to do all in your power to avoid temptation, starting with controls on your computer
5	accountability to others	a community of Christians who are holding you accountable and supporting you in your struggle

So what stops you from confessing to someone else?

WHICH DO YOU VALUE MORE: YOUR HOLINESS OR YOUR REPUTATION?

"My reputation will be shot to pieces." "What will people say?" "My ministry will be over." If this is what you're saying, then reputation and ministry have themselves become idols to you. If they prevent you dealing with sin in your life, then they've grown too important. They matter more than your holiness and God's glory. And that's a definition of idolatry, the fountain of all sin. If you won't seek accountability, then you love your reputation more than the glory of God. Or you trust yourself more than God. Or both.

You may say that confessing to another person is unnecessary because you've confessed your sin to God. And yes, it's true that Jesus is our only Mediator. But it's also true that Jesus has given us the Christian community to help us live for him. So ask yourself this: Why are you happy to confess your sin to God, but not to a human being? Could it be that you fear their opinion? Think about that for a moment. You're more concerned about the opinion of a human being than the opinion of God. You fear humans more than you fear God. The Bible repeatedly encourages us to help one another walk in holiness. Why are you spurning this help? Because the approval of other people matters more to you than overcoming your sin. Being thought of as holy matters more than actually being holy. "I have heard people tell me many times," says Steve Gallagher, "that they do not have anyone to confess to. What they were really saying is that they were not desperate enough to seek out someone that might be able to assist them."[9]

This is why confession to another person is so important. It's an act that signals and reinforces your real commitment to purity. "He who conceals his sins does not prosper, but whoever confesses and renounces them finds mercy" (Proverbs 28:13). David White of Harvest USA says:

> Every individual who comes to Harvest USA is different. The histories, life experiences, specifics of their sin and temptation, etc., are widely divergent and require particular attention. In short, there are not many universals—healing comes in specific ways, as diverse as our personal brokenness. In six years at the ministry, there is only one thing that clearly is universal: those committed to ruthless honesty consistently overcome their sin and make great strides in holiness. In stark contrast, I have never encountered an individual that overcame sexual

struggles if they were unwilling to bring the sin fully into the light, with an ever-increasing number of individuals. Those who refuse this path of ruthless honesty stay stuck in their sin or return to it after a short period of "white-knuckled" abstinence.[10]

Use discretion when you tell people. I often tell leaders, "Tell everyone you struggle; tell some people what you struggle with." Telling everyone will be unhelpful, especially when it comes to porn. Some people might choose to interpret your confession as giving an excuse for their own use. So confide in mature, godly people. Don't choose people whom you can manipulate.

TELLING YOUR WIFE

Tell your wife or girlfriend. "Confessing all to my wife," says Jack, "was very effective in cutting out my use of Internet porn."

You may say, "But I don't want to hurt her." Then why are you looking at pornography? I suspect the reality is that you don't want to be shamed before her or risk her rejection. But you must tell her. You're already hurting her.

Don't tell your wife all the details. You need to be clear about what you've done, so she can offer forgiveness and help you in your ongoing struggle. Tell her *clearly* what you have done *in general*. You might say something like, "I've looked at porn on the Internet several times a month for the last two years." But there's no need to describe the specific things you've seen or done. And tell her everything up front. Avoid the temptation to tell her some things now and other things later, after she's gotten used to the idea. That will only create mistrust in her mind. She'll start to wonder what else you've not told her.

Your wife may assume it's her fault: *If only I'd loved him more or better*, she might think. *If only I'd had more or better sex with him.* You'll need to explain how you think porn works for you—what it provides that you lack—so she realizes that it's not simply about sex. Above all, take responsibility for your problem—don't subtly pass it off on her. Here's Trev's advice:

If you are married, my number one advice would be that you must tell your wife. Look at it like this. What you're involved with now is slowly, quietly, in dark places and corners, destroying your marriage. I was terrified about telling my wife—the shame, the embarrassment. What about the kids? What if she won't like me any more? But honestly it was the best thing I could have done. I feel now that a dark, black secret that had been eating away at our marriage has been exposed to the light and glare of day and it has lost its power. It's been an incredibly difficult and stressful time, but I feel stronger and more secure in my marriage, and so stronger and braver in my service of God than I can ever remember.

HELPING ONE ANOTHER CHANGE

Accountability is not always easy to find! "Accountability? Hah! Where does that come from around here?" writes Craig. Others agree. "I can't find accountability—none at all! In my experience, pornography is never talked about in any Christian context." "When I've spoken to friends about it, they either don't understand the problem or are in it worse than I am."

Let me address more directly those helping others struggling with porn. You may be in both categories—both struggling with porn yourself and helping others in a mutually supportive partnership.

A CULTURE OF GRACE

We have a cultural problem in many church circles. "I desperately want help," says Brian, "but I'm afraid of losing my spouse and ministry." Gregg puts it like this:

> There's rarely a place where men feel they can confess and be treated appropriately. I knew other men in seminary were struggling, but none of us would talk about it because we'd be pushed to the side rather than walked with in a relationship through the struggle to victory. Churches need to do a better job of becoming

communities of grace. Otherwise sin just stays hidden and grows and propagates and destroys Christ's beautiful bride.

We need to offer one another real grace. Don't leave people in their sin. Embody grace to people in the way you show acceptance and love. Brett writes, "You don't have to have done porn to be able to relate, you just have to be aware of your own deeply engrained sin issues and the amazing grace of God that reaches you still. Therein lies the key for engaging with the person struggling with porn. Be a presence, be sensitive, be strong where needed, but more than anything just be there."

Above all, point people to the God of grace. Give them hope. Set them free. No one should be left feeling condemned, because there is no condemnation for those who are in Christ Jesus. "If someone is confiding in you," says Dale, "*please* don't say, 'You've been doing *what?*' and run a mile. That person has taken a big step in telling you, and you have the responsibility of encouraging them to bring this area of their life to God—and then the joy of seeing God's transforming power in action."

Our churches often have a culture of performance instead of a culture of grace. Our meetings are accomplished, our ministry is professional, our presentations are faultless. This is a tough environment for a porn user. It makes it hard to open up. Moreover, porn is about performance. And if you don't feel you're matching up to the performance culture, porn will be a tempting alternative—a world where you always perform. "Confession was very tough at first because of the performance mentality I experienced at church. It wasn't cool to be seen to have problems and so I resolved to deal with things myself."

Dietrich Bonhoeffer says:

> It is possible that Christians may remain lonely in spite of daily worship together, prayer together, and all their community through service—that the final breakthrough to community does not occur precisely because they enjoy community with one another as pious believers, but not with one another as

those lacking piety, as sinners. For the pious community per-
mits no one to be a sinner. Hence all have to conceal their sins
from themselves and from the community. We are not allowed
to be sinners.[11]

There's a good chance that when you finally confess to someone
else, they may turn out to be struggling with the same issue. You can
still provide accountability even if you yourself continue to struggle
with porn. Don't wait until you're perfect before you help others! Not
only is that impossible to achieve, but "perfect" people tend to wit-
ness to their own good works rather than to the grace of God.

A CULTURE OF CONFRONTATION
Offer grace, but don't offer cheap grace.

I told others about my habit. It was a cry for help. But no one
really seems to check up on me.

Accountability has been really helpful, although I wish they
called me up on it more often and regularly just asked straight
out, "Have you been looking at porn recently?'

Accountability has been a bit of a dead end, really. I've told
other men at various times, and each time we've agreed to ask
one another, but it's not once happened. I think even when we
have permission men don't like to ask.

As the previous quotes reveal, people struggling with porn are
often desperate for someone to be tough with them: to say it as it is.
"I think Christian accountability outside my relationship with my
wife is a joke," says Alex. "I've confessed my sin to every Christian
community I've been involved with. Most take it seriously, but haven't
a clue what to do from there. They usually pray for me and then it's
forgotten."

People often confess, but then sugarcoat their confession, down-
playing or excusing their sin. So be tough on one another. One leader
of an accountability group found the group made people feel better

about themselves. They might be struggling with porn, they reasoned, but they were in a group and so at least they were dealing with the problem. They could think of themselves as "recovering" porn addicts. He realized he needed to be more directive and confrontational. Everyone should leave their meetings motivated to battle against temptation. John says, "I've used accountability software. It's been a huge help, but only because the person who receives my reports will respond appropriately—strongly, but graciously."

TIPS FOR MUTUAL ACCOUNTABILITY AND AN ACCOUNTABILITY GROUP

Convene a porn-related group only for a limited period of time. Otherwise being in the group will encourage people to identify themselves by their sin, keeping their failure forever before their eyes. We need to define ourselves not as porn addicts or even ex–porn users, but as saints, children of God, brothers-in-arms.

A better alternative is to establish an accountability group that is not defined as a porn group. Invite everyone to identify their current top struggle. So the group is not a porn group, but someone struggling with porn can find accountability and support. Porn is always a symptom of deeper issues. It's about lust, but it's also about anger, intimacy, control, fear, escape and so on. Many of these problems will show up in other areas of a person's life. A group with a wider brief may find it easier to spot these connections.

It may be helpful to highlight some male bonding and male language. (I don't mean group hugs!) Many men don't want to sit around talking about their feelings, but they do yearn for camaraderie. Jonathan Dobson advocates "fight clubs"—"simple groups of 2-3 who meet regularly to help one another beat the flesh and believe in the promises of God." The three rules of the fight club are: (1) Know your sin. (2) Fight your sin. (3) Trust your Savior.[12]

Men also want to work with other men toward a common purpose. Listening to stories during the sixty-fifth anniversary of the Normandy landings, I was struck how—despite the horror of war and the loss of comrades—this was clearly the highlight in the lives of many of those involved. This was the moment when their lives had purpose. Meaningful companionship had been forged through common adversity.

So you might, for example, expand the work of your group to include wrestling together in prayer for the mission of your church. This builds that sense of camaraderie and refocuses attention away from self-preoccupation toward serving others. You might make it a common feature of your group that you do works of service together—clearing the garden of an elderly church member or decorating a room for newly married couple or organizing a neighborhood event.

It is important to ask *specific questions*. "How are you doing?" is simply too vague. Often we ask that kind of question because we don't really want to hear an honest answer—or we don't want to be asked a specific question in return. But general questions allow people to wriggle free from accountability. A student worker told me that a typical conversation with a young man goes something like this:

So how's your week been?
OK. Better than the last one, but not great.
Have you been reading your Bible and praying?
Yeah, but doesn't really seem to help much.
Anything else happening in your life?
No—you know, the same stuff.
Work going well for you?
Yeah, I really enjoy . . .
Been looking at porn this week?
Yeah, all the time.
Masturbating?
Yeah, can't stop.

He comments, "Unless I ask the specific question, the guys never open up." Explore with people what, when, how long and why, but also beware of questions that are too specific. "Have you viewed porn?" might elicit the response no, even though the person has watched sexual content on late-night television. It wasn't technically labeled as porn—they will reason—even though they watched it for sexual stimulation.

Here is a possible set of accountability questions:

Since we last met:

- How has God been speaking to you? What's God been doing in your life?

- What temptations have your faced, and what sins do you need to confess?

- Have you struggled with sexual temptation, porn or inappropriate fantasies?

- Have you given in to addictive behavior or escapism?

- Have any relationships been spoiled by your pride, anger, selfishness, fear or lack of forgiveness?

- Have you given time to prayer and the Word of God?

- What opportunities have you had to glorify Jesus through your words or actions?

These questions are deliberately not all focused on porn so that they will allow you to celebrate God's work in one another's lives.

You might want to agree on some goals as a group. For example:

Before our next meeting:

- I will not use porn or fantasize sexually.

- I will cultivate my love for God each day through prayer, praise and the Bible.

- If married, I will show appreciation to my wife and serve her each day.

- I will contact another member of the group to encourage him.[13]

People often struggle immediately after a group has met, because that represents the longest time before they will next experience accountability. So you may need to follow up with one another between meetings. You could, for example, send a text asking how someone is doing. Do the equivalent of random, on-the-spot drug testing!

Make confidentiality your normal practice, but don't promise it. The Bible warns us not to gossip (2 Corinthians 12:20). "A gossip betrays a confidence, but a trustworthy man keeps a secret" (Proverbs 11:13). So don't tell others what people have said within the group. Try to gain a reputation for being discreet.

But there are limits to confidentiality. We need to tell others when criminality is involved or where other people are threatened (Leviticus 5:1). We need to involve others when people are unrepentant (Matthew 18:15-17). Make yourself accountable to your church leaders for your conduct and be ready to seek their advice. If someone tells you about illegal behavior, particularly if children are involved, then you have a moral and legal obligation to pass on this information. If in doubt, check the website of your state's or province's Child Protection Services, or see the Child Welfare Information Gateway at www.childwelfare.gov/systemwide/laws_policies.

Above all, focus on Christ. It's your role to help one another trust in Christ, not to become an alternative to Christ. So beware of emotional dependency. Explore the details of what someone has been viewing only when this helps to identify the liberating truths about God that will counter the way porn works for that person. Don't merely satisfy your curiosity—that's not good for either of you.

Focus on the gospel—on good news. Accountability groups too easily revert to legalism in which we cajole one another into religious conformity. People can end up fighting sin because they fear the group's disapproval and not because they treasure Christ. Our message again and again must not be simply, "You should not use porn," but "You need not use porn because God offers more."

Don't give up on accountability, whether you're looking for it or providing it. It can sometimes be hard to find and hard to sustain. But it's an essential ingredient. Take hope from these stories:

Accountability has been a massive help. I first told another Christian about a year ago and that's the time it all changed, really. Other Christians have reacted graciously, discreetly and supportively.

Accountability has been patchy, but has been the most effective tool God has used to change me. Confession has always been two- or three-way, so the response has been mutual encouragement and support.

I have three very close accountability buddies—not just for porn but for our whole Christian walk. We are all in our late sixties and want to "finish well."

Accountability has played a huge role. My roommates and I all have dinner together every Sunday night and "spill our guts" to each other, confessing our sins and praying for one another. It's been very helpful.

How important has accountability been? Immeasurable! I need accountability! I use accountability software as I'm on the Internet so much. I meet with my minister and chat and confess even the little things. Secrecy is a killer with this addiction.

A LIFETIME OF DAILY CHANGE

Understanding doesn't equal change. So it's time to think: *What am I going to do now? What are my next steps?*

Only Christians are free not to sin, because we have new controlling desires from God. But the old sinful desires and habits linger on, so the Christian life is a battle, and the battlefield is our hearts. Change involves a lifetime of daily struggle. "The battle is never over," says Karl, "so beware lest you fall."

Daily change. "The only thing that worked for me was to commit to obeying God one day at a time." One day at time. That's the advice of many people who've struggled with porn. Soldiers can't take a day off in the midst of battle, and neither can you. "Understand that victory is on a day-by-day basis," says Bob. "Be aware of the temptation at all times, and have the grace of God as a constant source to remind you that you can achieve victory."

Lifelong change. Change takes a lifetime. That's because the habits of sin run deep. But it's also because God wants us to learn the depth of his grace. He's preparing us to praise his grace for all eternity! It's often hard going because he wants us to learn to grasp hold of Christ—firmly, desperately, humbly.

"It's a long-term struggle," says Dave, "and any thoughts that 'it's over' are a lie from the enemy. Think of little steps that can be made over the long-term." Brian's advice is similar: "I would say that first you have to recognize that it will be a lifelong battle. Take one day at a time."

People often long for instant victory—for the struggle to go away. But victory is not life without temptation—not in this life. In this life victory is struggling with temptation and consistently choosing obedience. And it means choosing obedience out of love for Jesus—not out of fear of being caught.

There will be setbacks. Then it's time to fight the fight of faith again. It's time to fight to believe that you're accepted by God through the work of Jesus so that you draw near to him for forgiveness and help, time to believe that God has given you his Spirit to transform your life so you don't lose hope and let yourself sink back into the pit of porn, time to believe that the glory of God and the promise of Christ are bigger and better and more enduring than the lies of porn.

5

Freed for the Glory of God

THE FRENCH WRITER ANTOINE DE Saint-Exupéry said, "If you want to build a ship, don't drum up people to collect wood, and don't assign them tasks and work, but rather teach them to long for the endless immensity of the sea."[1]

Warnings not to do something are rarely enough. Telling people the dangers of sin will take us only so far. What we need is a vision of the glory of Christ. When we desire Christ above all things, we'll root out sin in our lives with enthusiasm. Jesus said, "The kingdom of heaven is like treasure hidden in a field. When a man found it, he hid it again, and then in his joy went and sold all he had and bought that field" (Matthew 13:44). *In his joy* this man sold everything he owned. In our joy we'll root out porn in our lives to the extent that we have a vision of something better and bigger—if we have a vision for treasure more precious than porn.

We need to look beyond the frame not only to see the ugliness of porn (see chap. 1), but to get a biblical vision of beauty, sex, marriage, singleness and above all the glory of God.

Our first key ingredient in the battle against porn was *a hatred of porn itself (not just the shame it brings) and a longing for change.* Here's the other side of that ingredient: a vision of change, a vision of a different kind of life, a vision for God's glory.

1. A biblical vision of beauty. Our culture holds out a standard of beauty that is literally unattainable. The images that feed this vision of beauty are fake. Film star Julianne Moore recalled in an interview a friend looking at a glossy magazine. "Why don't I look like that?" exclaimed the friend. "Then she looked more closely. It *was* her. After the make-up staff had done their stuff, and the lighting man had weaved his magic, and perhaps above all when the photo had been brushed up with the latest software. The image wasn't real."[2] You can't look like people do in magazines and films because *they* don't look like that—not in real life! And this is not a neutral process—it's driven by commercial interests. Women are made to feel fat or ugly so they will buy dieting and beauty products.[3]

Not only that, but we're all constantly invited to assess one another. Magazines run features on who's looking best or on celebrities who got it wrong, pointing out their deficiencies. We've seen that we're invited to rank and rate women. We're all in a constant state of mutual evaluation and self-evaluation.

And what does this do for us all? According to research by Dove, only 2 percent of thousands of women from ten countries around the world consider themselves beautiful. Notions of beauty that are unattainable and unsustainable create a climate of dissatisfaction. Our partners cannot possibly hope to measure up to the expectation created in the media, especially as they grow older.

Not only is our ideal of beauty unattainable, it's also artificial. In our culture being tanned is considered beautiful. No one wants to be pasty and white. But in Solomon's time white skin was highly prized. The young woman in the Song of Songs says, "Dark am I, yet lovely. . . . Do not stare at me because I am dark" (Song 1:5-6). It's about wealth. The poor worked in the fields while the rich rested in the shade. Dark skin meant you were a peasant worker. Today dark skin means you can afford foreign holidays or can lounge in the sun. It's the same with body size. Westerners value thin women, Africans fat women. And then we layer on fashion—an ideal of appearance that changes from season to season.

The point is that our idea of beauty is shaped in significant measure by the culture around us. You may not look like a film star or a fashion model. But that doesn't mean you're not beautiful in your own way, or that you're undesirable. Your spouse may not look like a film star or a fashion model, but that doesn't mean you can't desire her.

Imagine a world in which our sense of beauty was not defined by the world around us. Imagine a world in which a young man never sees half-naked, provocative women on the billboards around town and in magazines; in which he doesn't see women being sexually suggestive, or simulated sex in movies; in which he's never looked at pornography on the Internet or movies or magazines; in which he's never met women showing their cleavage or their thighs or their underwear.

Now imagine him on his wedding night. His new bride comes to him. By the standards of our world she may or may not have a perfect body. But then this is not our world, and this is in fact the first time our young man has ever seen a naked woman. He thinks she's the most wonderful, exquisite creature on the planet. He looks on her with unqualified desire. He loves her with unqualified love.

Sadly, this is not our world, and we can't create it. But neither do we have to be passive. We don't have to conform to this world. We can be transformed by the renewing of our minds (Romans 12:2).

Choose to find your spouse beautiful. Don't think the catwalk and the screen define beauty and then assess your wife (or husband) by that standard. You can look at your wife as if she were the only woman you have ever seen.

I wonder if you ever think, *Her breasts are too small or too large. Her legs are too fat or too thin. Her stomach is no longer flat. Her face is getting wrinkled. She's not as beautiful as she once was.* Says who? What's the standard against which you decide this? Your wife or husband will grow old. And if "young" is your definition of beauty, then they'll look less beautiful.

But it doesn't need to be that way. Who says a flat stomach is the epitome of beauty? Why can't you find curves attractive? Who says

wrinkles are ugly? Why can't you find wrinkles attractive? Pastor
Mark Driscoll writes:

> Eve may or may not have been beautiful, but to Adam she was
> glorious because she was all he had ever known. Practically, he
> had no standard of beauty to compare his bride to—she was his
> only standard of beauty. In creation, we see the wise pattern
> that for every man his standard of beauty is not to be objecti-
> fied, but rather it should simply be his wife. This means that if
> a man has a tall, skinny red-headed wife then that is sexy for
> him, and if his neighbor has a short, curvy brunette wife then
> that is sexy for him.
>
> Pornographic lust exists to elicit coveting and dissatisfaction
> that no woman can satisfy because she cannot be tall and short,
> endowed and waifish, black and white, young and old, like the
> harem laid out in pornography.[4]

Wisdom says,

> Rejoice in the wife of your youth.
> She is a loving deer, a graceful doe.
> Let her breasts satisfy you always.
> May you always be captivated by her love. (Proverbs 5:18-19 NLT)

It's a choice—a command. It's wisdom: to find your wife beautiful, to
enjoy her breasts and not to wish they were bigger, smaller, younger
or someone else's.

And it's not a hard command. It is, after all, a command to fondle
your wife's breasts! It's a command to enjoy your wife, and—in a
culture in which we choose our wives—we're not being asked to
find someone beautiful whom we think is ugly. We're being asked
to continue finding someone beautiful whom we already think is
beautiful.

Make your spouse feel beautiful. "Don't stare at me because I am
dark," says the beloved in the Song of Songs, "the sun has darkened
my skin" (Song 1:6 NLT). She was dark-skinned in an age that valued

white skin. She's had to labor in the vineyards, so she hasn't had the time to care for her appearance ("my own vineyard"). She feels self-conscious compared with the sophisticated daughters of Jerusalem, so she asks them not to stare at her.

Compare this with how she speaks at the end of the Song:

> I was a virgin, like a wall;
> > now my breasts are like towers.
> When my lover looks at me,
> > he is delighted with what he sees. (Song 8:10 NLT)

His love makes her feel beautiful. She welcomes his stares! She puffs out her chest to her lover, for his love makes her feel secure, wanted, desirable. If your husband (or wife) says you're beautiful, then you *are* beautiful in the eyes of everyone who matters. "But you're biased," your wife may respond when you say she's beautiful. But so too are the advertisers! They want her to feel ugly, so she purchases their products.

I believe people look their most beautiful when they smile. So when people look in the mirror with self-critical eyes they don't see beauty. But when I look at my wife with love and she smiles back at me, she looks so beautiful.

Value inward beauty above outward beauty. "Don't be concerned about the outward beauty," says Peter, "of fancy hairstyles, expensive jewelry, or beautiful clothes. You should clothe yourselves instead with the beauty that comes from within, the unfading beauty of a gentle and quiet spirit, which is so precious to God" (1 Peter 3:3-4 NLT).

Outward beauty is expensive. But inner beauty is precious. It's something money can't buy. Even when it goes unnoticed by other people, it is precious in God's sight. A person whose priority is outward beauty will be preoccupied with him- or herself: How do I look? What am I eating? But if your priority is inner beauty, then your preoccupation will be with God: What does God think? What will bring him glory? How can I trust him more? This is the beauty we should esteem.

If you're attracted to someone by their inner beauty, then you'll always be attracted to her. Outward beauty fades (2 Corinthians 4:16). Not even plastic surgery can prevent the aging process. Things start to sag. Lines start to form. But inner beauty is unfading. It doesn't diminish with age. Indeed, if the Holy Spirit is at work in our lives, then inner beauty grows. My wife grows more beautiful to me as time goes on.

Many of us look at our bodies without mercy, or we look critically at the bodies of other people without mercy. Too fat—too thin—too many spots—big nose—double chin—small breasts. No latitude— no mercy. But God looks at our bodies with mercy. Paul says, "Therefore, I urge you, brothers, in view of God's mercy, to offer your bodies as living sacrifices, holy and pleasing to God—this is your spiritual act of worship" (Romans 12:1). Many of us make sacrifices to gain the perfect body: going without food we love; taking exercise we dislike. We want good-looking bodies that please women—or men. In so doing we worship the god of sex or approval or pleasure. The Bible calls us to a different kind of sacrifice: to offer our bodies to God as an act of worship to him.[5] It calls us to have bodies that please God—not because of what they look like but because of what they do in his service. This is the beauty we should esteem.

2. *A biblical vision of sexuality.* "Porn has affected the way I view sex and sexuality," says Dave. "I struggle with the biblical concept of sex as a God-given gift for marriage, rather than as a sinful act in itself." Titus 1:15 says, "To the pure, all things are pure, but to those who are corrupted and do not believe, nothing is pure. In fact, both their minds and consciences are corrupted." In the hands of the porn industry, sex becomes this horrible, ugly, corrupted thing. *But* to the pure it can still be pure.

In our culture sex is everything and sex is nothing. On the one hand, sex is everything and everywhere. It's used to sell products. The media talk incessantly about the sex lives of celebrities. Fashion encourages people to parade their bodies in ways that signal sexual availability. To be "enlightened" about sex in our culture has become a strange topsy-turvy euphemism for immorality.

But as sex has spread everywhere, it has spread very thinly. It has lost its significance, its power, its mystery. "An ever-increasing craving for an ever-diminishing pleasure": that's how C. S. Lewis suggests the devil ensnares people with pleasure.[6] And that's a description of sex in our culture.

Sex is God's good creation. This is how the Song of Songs begins: "This is Solomon's song of songs, more wonderful than any other" (Song 1:1 NLT). Under the reign of King Solomon there was a great period of learning, wisdom, poetry and literature. And from this golden age in Israel's history, this song is "more wonderful than any other." And what are the opening words of this best of songs? "Kiss me" (Song 1:2 NLT). And what are the next words? "Kiss me again."

Chapter 3 of the Song describes the wedding of the young man and woman. She arrives in a haze of perfume (v. 6). He arrives escorted by his friends with great ceremony, as if he is King Solomon himself (vv. 7-11). And then in chapter 4 we move into the honeymoon suite. With intense, erotic poetry he describes her body, her eyes, her hair, her mouth, her neck, her breasts. "You are my private garden, my treasure, my bride, a secluded spring, a hidden fountain" (Song 4:12 NLT). In other words, she's virgin—a private garden that no one has entered. "Your thighs shelter a paradise of pomegranates with rare spices" (Song 4:13 NLT). He's talking about her vagina— that's what is sheltered in her thighs—but the language is tender and gentle, not crude or aggressive. She responds, "Come into your garden, my love; taste its finest fruits" (Song 4:16 NLT). It's an invitation to enter her physically, to have intercourse with her. Before they were married the refrain was to "not awaken love until the time is right" (Song 2:7; 3:5 NLT). The same word is used here, but now the time is right. Now it's an invitation to make love: awake, rise up, come into your garden.

"I have entered my garden, my treasure, my bride!" (Song 5:1 NLT). No one has previously entered her, tasted her, drunk from her delights. But now her lover enters her garden, gathers her myrrh, eats her honey, drinks her wine. There are 111 lines before this verse and 111 lines after it. This is the centerpiece. This is the climax—in every way! This Song of Songs, the epitome of wisdom, has at its heart a celebration of sexual intercourse. Ben Patterson says: "Sex is good because the God who created sex is good. And God is glorified greatly when we receive his gift with thanksgiving and enjoy it the way he meant for it to be enjoyed."[7] To think negatively about sex is ingratitude toward God. It is to impugn God's goodness. It is, according to 1 Timothy 4:1-5, the teaching of demons!

Our sexuality is supposed to be like Niagara Falls. The rocks constrain the water, forcing it into a powerful surging rush. Porn makes sexuality like the Mississippi Delta. The water there is not constrained by anything. It's spread out wide and thin and muddy. The Bible gives us safeguards, not to protect us from sex but to protect sex from us, not to stop us being spoiled by sex but to stop sex being spoiled by us!

God made the world from nothing except his word, nothing except his imagination. He wasn't limited by his materials. The messy business of sex, with bodily fluids and hormones and dangerous passions, wasn't simply the best he could do in the circumstances. God conceived in his mind a perfect world and it was a world with sex. Sex is good.

Not only that, but the Song of Songs is part of what we call the "wisdom tradition" of the Bible. Sex is good, and it is wisdom to pursue, encourage and nurture an intimate, pleasurable sexual relationship.

Sex is an act of unification. So what is sex for? It is, first and foremost, an act of unification, uniting two people into one flesh. Sex is designed by God to complete or fulfill or bind together the companionship of marriage. So sex is very powerful. It's not simply a pleasurable pastime. It creates a new reality. Sex makes two people one (Genesis 2:24). And it does so at the deepest of levels. It's not only a physical act but a spiritual act.

Jesus adds a further level. Quoting Genesis 2, he says: "'This explains why a man leaves his father and mother and is joined to his wife, and the two are united into one.' Since they are no longer two but one, let no one split apart what God has joined together" (Mark 10:7-9 NLT). Who unites people through sex? Not merely the man and woman involved, but God himself. When a married couple have sex, God is at work, uniting them, making them one flesh.

So sex is not just about satisfying physical urges or getting physical pleasure. Sex binds you to your partner, and that bond is as enduring as the grave (Song of Songs 8:6-7). You can no more untie the bonds that sex creates than you can bring people back from the grave. The feelings that sex creates cannot be quenched even by many waters.

That's why porn—along with all sex outside of marriage—is a sham, a fiction, a lie. You can no more "try out" sex than you can "try out" birth. The very act produces a new reality that cannot be undone.

Sex is an act of disclosure. Knowing in the Bible is a metaphor for sex. This isn't because the writers were coy but because sex really is about knowing. Why did Adam and Eve feel no shame though they were naked? Genesis 2:24 suggests it was because they were naked in the context of covenant love. They felt free to disclose themselves because they were confident their disclosure would be met with love.

But what happens when sin enters the situation? "At that moment their eyes were opened, and they suddenly felt shame at their nakedness. So they sewed fig leaves together to cover themselves" (Genesis 3:7 NLT).

First, they felt shame because of their fear of each other. When you take off your clothes, you're vulnerable to jokes, rude remarks and scorn; to assault, hurt and defilement. In the context of covenant love, that's not a problem. You trust the other person not to hurt you because they've promised to love you. And we glimpse that in marriage: in that context people can be naked without fear.

But Adam and Eve became covenant-breakers. They've broken

their covenant with God and rejected his love. So now they can't trust each other to be faithful to their covenant of love. They can't be confident that the other will not exploit or abuse their nakedness. Their instinct is now to cover themselves. Sex really works only in the context of covenant love.

Second, the reason for this shame is that Adam and Eve now have something to hide. When you remove your clothes, you expose not only your body but your heart. Before the fall into sin Adam and Eve had nothing to hide. But now they cover their bodies as a sign that sin has shamed their hearts. That's why nudity, naturism, flashing and exhibitionism are all wrong: they're a denial that we have any reason to feel shame, a denial that anything has changed, a denial of our sin.

The good news is that God covers our shame with clothing. "The LORD God made garments of skin for Adam and his wife and clothed them" (Genesis 3:21). And this act points to the perfect righteousness of Christ with which God covers our inner shame.

Sexual icons. Our sexual icons should not be half-naked young guys with six-packs or 36-24-36 women simpering in lingerie. Those icons are fantasies. People only look like that with the help of Photoshop software. These images don't show what the people look like first thing in the morning, still less what their hearts are like.

Let me suggest that a better "sexual icon" would be an elderly couple celebrating their wedding anniversary. This is the truth about sex and marriage. This is sex in a context that points to the meaning of sex and marriage—God's covenant love for his people.

Of course none of us can remove ourselves from our sexualized world. Those of us who've used porn can't wind the clock back and regain a preporn view of women. But we *can* stop feeding a pornified view of women and sex. We can begin to replace a pornified view with a biblical view. We can be transformed by the renewing of our minds (Romans 12:2). We may never entirely eradicate our memories of porn in this life, but if we stop feeding them and replace them with a biblical vision, they will fade into the background. We're not alone in this movement. God gives his Holy Spirit to change our hearts and renew our vision. Many men I know have regained a healthy, wholesome view of sex with the help of the Spirit. Listen to Andrew's testimony:

> The most valuable thing in my life was preaching from the Song of Songs. Meditating on those Scriptures and seeing a biblical understanding of the joy and delight in the self-giving of godly and pure sexual intimacy made it so obvious how disgusting every other perversion was. It was a transformation of my thinking that preceded a change in my behavior. And it wasn't just seeing the biblical understanding of the sex ethic, but seeing how it was ultimately Christ-centered.

3. A biblical vision of marriage. Survey after survey shows that married couples have more sex and better sex: better than cohabiting couples and far better than single people.[8] It's hardly surprising: learning what pleases another person takes time and practice and commitment. Yet our culture almost universally portrays the opposite. In films and television programs single people have fantastic sex while married couples have dull sex—if they have sex at all. A University of Chicago study found that married couples in movies are rarely depicted having a great sex life.[9] Marriage is often seen as the end of love. We have thousands of songs about falling in love and out of love. Very few celebrate staying in love.

One of the things that porn does is to make us think marriage is for sex. But it's the other way round: sex is for marriage. God created sex to bind couples together in marital love and faithfulness. We need a bigger vision for marriage.

A picture of God's covenant love. The covenant of marriage is an echo of God's covenant relationship with his people (Ezekiel 16:8) and the unfaithfulness of God's people is described as adultery (Hosea 2:2-13). But God also promises to take his people as his wife again (Hosea 2:14-23; Jeremiah 31:31-32; Ephesians 5:25-27, 31-32). So the Bible story ends with a marriage. God's new world is described as a wedding feast for the marriage between God's people and God's Son (Revelation 19:9).

Sexuality and marriage were given by God to show us the nature of his passionate love for his people. So whatever our experience of marriage, sex or singleness, our sexuality helps us understand God's relationship with his people. If we've experienced the joy of marriage, then we know something of the joy of companionship with God. If we've experienced the pain of singleness, then we know something of the need for God that human beings have. If we've experienced the pain of betrayal or if sex is associated for us with hurt, then we know something of God's holy jealousy for the love of his people. If we've had any experience of passion, whether requited or unrequited, we know something of the passion of God for his people.

Marriage is a covenant of love. Covenant isn't a word we use very often. The nearest word we have today is *contract*. This captures the sense that in marriage we make promises that are solemn and binding. In most cultures those promises are actually legally binding. The problem is that *contract* sounds like a business deal! It lacks the sense of love and relationship and friendship. That's why *covenant* is a better word. A covenant is a contract plus love. The Bible has a special word for it: *hesed,* "covenant love" or "steadfast love." It's used to describe human fidelity, but also to describe God's covenant love for his people—a love to which he has bound himself through his word. Our faithfulness in marriage is modeled on God's faithfulness to us. Listen to the Song of Songs 8:6-7 (using one alternative translation from a footnote):

Place me like a seal over your heart,
    like a seal on your arm.
For love is as strong as death,
    its passion as enduring as the grave.
Love flashes like fire,
    the brightest kind of flame.
Many waters cannot quench love,
    nor can rivers drown it.
If a man tried to buy love

with all his wealth,
    his offer would be utterly scorned. (NLT)

The great thing about marriage is that combination of binding
promises and loving relationship. Here is a love as strong as death,
but it's also a love that is publicly sealed (v. 6). Here is love, but here
too is a wedding ring to remind the lovers of their covenant promises,
for those binding promises protect the loving relationship.

Porn is easy. It's trouble-free and its pleasures are instant. Marriage is hard work. It involves two sinners being thrown together in
close proximity! There are bound to be irritations, conflicts and
tough choices. Love as an act of will makes those tough choices. But
the making of those choices itself creates love as an affection. I feel
more in love with my wife now than I did twenty years ago when we
were first married. The feeling has grown and intensified. And the
reason is that, again and again, we have chosen to love each other.
The accumulation of those choices makes a strong bond—a bond
that porn can never replicate or even imitate.

Marriage is a covenant of companionship. A covenant of love describes the nature of marriage. But what of its purpose? What is marriage *for*?

Some Christians have said that the defining purpose of marriage
is for procreation. They stress the command to the first man and
woman to "be fruitful and multiply" (Genesis 1:28). And yes, marriage is the God-given context in which to nurture children. But marriage is for more than procreation. Otherwise childless marriages
would be lesser marriages, and marriages would be redundant once
children had left home. The Song of Songs, the Bible's great celebration of married love, never mentions children. Nor does this view
serve children well. If their parents' marriage revolves around them,
then children grow up thinking they're the center of the world.

Other Christians have said that marriage is for protection. They
emphasize 1 Corinthians 7:9: "It's better to marry than to burn with
lust" (NLT). Again, it's true that marriage is the proper context for

sexuality to find expression in intercourse. But marriage was given before humanity fell into sin. It's not just a way of coping with our sinful desires. If this is your view of marriage, then you don't really want a wife or husband! You just want sex. There's no real commitment to your spouse and only a legalistic commitment to marriage. Your real commitment is to sex.

The true purpose for marriage is given in Genesis 2:18: "The LORD God said, 'It is not good for the man to be alone. I will make a helper suitable for him.' " Marriage is for companionship ("It is not good for the man to be alone") and for service ("I will make a helper suitable for him").

God declares creation very good (Genesis 1:31). But there's one thing that is not good: it's not good for man to be alone. Marriage was God's idea. God himself frames this solution to man's aloneness. God himself is the first Father to give away a bride: "he brought her to the man" (Genesis 2:22).

In the Song of Songs 8:10 the woman says: "I was in his eyes as one who brings out peace" (ESV, using alternative footnote). The word *peace* is the Hebrew *shalom*. It means rest and contentment, wholeness and completeness. In Song of Songs 6:13 she is his "Shulammite." There is no known place named Shulam. It probably means "his girl of shalom" or "his shalom-bringing girl." She gives him rest and makes him complete.

Why a woman? Why not another man? Adam's cry of joy at seeing Eve ("At last, bone of my bone, and flesh of my flesh") reminds us that this companionship is expressed in sexual intercourse. Only sexuality creates passions sufficient to illustrate God's passionate love for his people. Friendship alone is not enough to teach us the nature of God's relationship with his people. That requires the ecstasy and passion of sex (and sometimes the pain and betrayal of sex gone wrong).

Marriage is a covenant of service. Genesis 2:18 suggests a second purpose for marriage: "The Lord God said, 'It is not good for the man to be alone. I will make a helper suitable for him.' " Marriage is not to be self-serving and indulgent. It's not all about my emotional desires.

Marriage is one context in which we can express our need to give, serve and love another.

More than that, man and woman are partners in the task God has given humanity. The task of imaging God, reflecting his glory, ruling creation and filling the earth is given to humanity, male and female (Genesis 1:26-28). With the story of sin and redemption the task takes a new turn. We become involved in the work of *re*-creation. We work together to proclaim good news of reconciliation.

Some people will serve God best as single people (Matthew 19:12; 1 Corinthians 7:32-35). But many will serve God in the partnership of marriage. If you're married, then your marriage is to be a partnership of service. That doesn't mean you will always serve together, but it does mean you support each other in your service of God. Your marriage is not your own. It's not there to satisfy your sexual desires. Marriage is a gift for service, and sex is gloriously given to cement that partnership. But don't let sex become the goal of your marriage—otherwise porn may seem like a good supplement. Your marriage belongs to God. It's to be offered to him, consecrated for his glory.

4. A biblical vision of singleness. Of course, a biblical vision of sexuality and marriage is all very well if you're married. But it doesn't seem to offer much help for those who are single. Married men struggle with porn just as much as single men, if not more. But single people still commonly long for marital and sexual intimacy. Porn may seem a poor substitute, but at least it's something. It's very easy for those who feel "cursed" with singleness to justify using porn as some sort of compensation.

We need a biblical vision of singleness. Churches don't always help. There was a time when the church saw marriage as second best—the spiritual best was monasteries, convents and a celibate clergy. But today evangelical churches more often seem to view singleness as second best.

There are strong reasons for marriage. In Genesis 2 we saw that God's response to man's "aloneness" is to make a woman. Men and women are literally made to live together in marriage. So in the Old

Testament marriage was seen as the norm.

But there is another, bigger reason why marriage was the norm in the Old Testament. The whole story of salvation after humanity's rebellion begins with God's call to Abraham (Genesis 12:2-3). God promises salvation to the world through the offspring of Abraham and promises a name for Abraham through his family.

That family became the people of Israel. And in Israel offspring mattered. Through the offspring of Israel God was going to save the world. You had a name among God's people and a part in God's plan by having offspring. So King Saul says to David, "Swear to me therefore by the LORD that you will not cut off my offspring after me, and that you will not destroy my name out of my father's house" (1 Samuel 24:21 ESV). Under the Levirate marriage system the wife of a deceased man would marry his brother and their first son would carry the dead man's name, so that his name lived on. When Boaz marries the widow Ruth, he says: "I have acquired Ruth, the Moabite widow of Mahlon, to be my wife. This way she can have a son to carry on the family name of her dead husband and to inherit the family property here in his hometown. You are all witnesses today" (Ruth 4:10 NLT).

Singleness was therefore a source of grief. When the daughter of Jephthah is to be killed, she asks for two months to grieve, not—as we might imagine—her imminent death but her virginity (Judges 11:37). She will be left without descendants, without a place in Israel's history and without a name.

There are good reasons for singleness. With this in mind, listen to the words of Isaiah. Isaiah has spoken of God's Servant suffering in the place of his people: "He was pierced for our rebellion, crushed for our sins," says Isaiah, talking about Jesus (Isaiah 53:5). Now he bursts out:

> Sing, O childless woman,
> you who have never given birth!
> Break into loud and joyful song, O Jerusalem,
> you who have never been in labor.
> For the desolate woman now has more children

than the woman who lives with her husband," says the LORD.

Fear not; you will no longer live in shame.
  Don't be afraid; there is no more disgrace for you.
You will no longer remember the shame of your youth
  and the sorrows of widowhood.
For your Creator will be your husband;
  the LORD of Heaven's Armies is his name!
He is your Redeemer, the Holy One of Israel,
  the God of all the earth. (54:1, 4-5 NLT)

Because of what Jesus will do, the single woman and the barren woman have a reason to sing. For they will have more children than the woman who lives with her husband. The death of Jesus will produce "offspring" and they will be "many" (Isaiah 53:10-11). Moreover, God himself will be a husband, taking away the shame of the single woman.

Or listen to Isaiah 56:3-5. Here God addresses eunuchs:

Don't let the eunuchs say,
  "I'm a dried-up tree with no children and no future."
For this is what the LORD says:
"I will bless those eunuchs
  who keep my Sabbath days holy
and who choose to do what pleases me
  and commit their lives to me.
I will give them—within the walls of my house—
  a memorial and a name
  far greater than sons and daughters could give.
For the name I give them is an everlasting one.
  It will never disappear! (NLT)

Single people say, "I have no children and no future." But God says, "I will give you a name—an everlasting name. And I will give a reward far greater than children."

That's because now, through Jesus, being part of God's people and part of God's future doesn't depend on marriage or children. When Jesus' mother and brothers come for him, he asks, " 'Who is my mother? Who are my brothers?' Then he looked at those around him and said, 'Look, these are my mother and brothers. Anyone who does God's will is my brother and sister and mother' " (Mark 3:33-35 NLT).

Marriage illustrates some great truths about God's covenant love for his people. But, after Jesus, singleness now also illustrates some great truths about God's salvation. It reminds us all

1. That the family of God grows not by propagation through sexual intercourse, but by regeneration through faith in Christ;

2. That relationships in Christ are more permanent, and more precious, than relationships in families; . . .

3. That marriage is temporary, and finally gives way to the relationship to which it was pointing all along: Christ and the church—the way a picture is no longer needed when you see face to face;

4. That faithfulness to Christ defines the value of life; all other relationships get their final significance from this. No family relationship is ultimate; relationship to Christ is.[10]

All the good reasons for getting married are still there. But now there are also good reasons for remaining single. Jesus says, "Some choose not to marry for the sake of the Kingdom of Heaven. Let anyone accept this who can" (Matthew 19:12 NLT). Jesus himself did not marry.

Nor did Paul. He says, "I wish everyone were single, just as I am. But God gives to some the gift of marriage, and to others the gift of singleness. So I say to those who aren't married and to widows—it's better to stay unmarried, just as I am" (1 Corinthians 7:7-8 NLT). He explains why:

I want you to be free from the concerns of this life. An unmarried man can spend his time doing the Lord's work and thinking how to please him. But a married man has to think about his earthly responsibilities and how to please his wife. His interests are divided. In the same way, a woman who is no longer married or has never been married can be devoted to the Lord and holy in body and in spirit. But a married woman has to think about her earthly responsibilities and how to please her husband. (1 Corinthians 7:32-34 NLT)

Singleness brings its own opportunities to serve God. It enables you to do things that married people either can't do or can't do fully.

So Paul calls marriage a gift *and* he calls singleness a gift. Some of you may feel singleness is an unwanted gift! It feels like the orange jumper your grandmother gave you at Christmas that you'll never wear. But God invites you to see it as a gift, an opportunity to serve and delight in God. God offers you a gift "far greater than sons and daughters could give" (Isaiah 56:5 NLT). Will you accept his gift?

Don't live as a not-yet-married person or a left-on-the-shelf person. Do not "cope" with singleness, as if singleness were some kind of illness. Live as a person gifted by God with singleness. Grasp the opportunities it brings with enthusiasm. The question you need to ask is not, "God, why have you not given me a spouse?" but, "God, what are you doing with and through my singleness?"[11]

A little later in 1 Corinthians, Paul says, "A spiritual gift is given to each of us so we can help each other" or "for the common good" (1 Corinthians 12:7 NLT; see also 1 Peter 4:10). It's the same word that Paul uses to describe the gift of singleness. Your singleness is not your own. It's not an identity, an excuse or a bitterness that belongs to you. It's given to you to serve others, to be used to bless God and his people. (The same is true of marriage: it's not your marriage but a gift given to you to serve your spouse, your children and the church.)

So how do you decide whether you have the "gift of singleness"? How do you decide whether you can best serve God single or married? If you're single, then you have the gift of singleness! Singleness is not some mystical calling. It's the circumstances in which you find yourself. It may or may not mean you will always be single. But while you are single, see it as an opportunity to serve God. A decision to stop being single will then be determined by your opportunities for service and your opportunities for marriage!

"It is not good for man to be alone," said God. Marriage was the first solution to this aloneness, but not the only solution. The church is to be family for singles. My observation is that living alone can make people self-indulgent because they have to please only themselves. Self-indulgence is fertile soil for porn. So share your life with other people. If possible, share your home with someone else. Don't shut yourself away in the evenings, thereby creating the perfect conditions to be tempted to use porn. Seek out the Christian community. And if you are married, be open and hospitable. Remember marriage is a covenant of service. We can't be substitute husbands and wives, but we can be brothers and sisters. The church family gives single people children. It offers companionship, opportunities to serve others and care in old age. "God sets the lonely in families," says the psalmist in Psalm 68:6.

5. *A biblical vision of God's glory.* A life without porn can renew your relationship to women, to your wife or to your future wife. But even more important, it can renew your relationship with God.

Proverbs warns us against adulterous sex and calls us instead to "drink water from your own cistern" (Proverbs 5:15). Thinking about your wife as a water tank might not seem the most compelling metaphor! But in the hot climate experienced by the readers of Proverbs, the cool water contained in deep wells was a powerful picture of refreshment, satisfaction and pleasure. Think of a glass of cool lemonade on a hot summer's day.

The same image is used of our relationship with God. God says:

My people have committed two sins:
They have forsaken me,

the spring of living water,
and have dug their own cisterns,
broken cisterns that cannot hold water. (Jeremiah 2:13)

God is the cool, living water that satisfies and refreshes us. Porn is a broken cistern that cannot hold water and cannot satisfy in any lasting way.

Truly God is good to Israel,
to those whose hearts are pure.
But as for me, I almost lost my footing.
My feet were slipping, and I was almost gone.
For I envied the proud
when I saw them prosper despite their wickedness.
(Psalm 73:1-3 NLT)

The psalmist is thrown into turmoil by the way unbelievers seem to do so well in life. This may be the way you feel about sex and marriage. You may see friends getting married—or you see friends getting lots of sex. People may laugh at your commitment to purity. You may think they're not really happy, but they look pretty happy! And so you conclude, as the psalmist does in verse 13, "Did I keep my heart pure for nothing? Did I keep myself innocent for no reason?" "I have been saying no to porn and sex, but God has not delivered the spouse I want or the sex I want."

This is how the psalmist thinks, until he comes into God's presence (v. 17). In God's presence he see the ultimate destiny of the wicked—they're on a slippery road, heading for the cliff of destruction (v. 18). The perspective of eternity enables the psalmist to make this lovely declaration:

Whom have I in heaven but you?
I desire you more than anything on earth.
My health may fail, and my spirit may grow weak,
but God remains the strength of my heart;
he is mine forever. (Psalm 73:25-26 NLT)

Is God enough for you in your singleness? Do you feel as if you need to be married to be complete? If God is *not* enough for you, then you are creating hopes for a spouse that no one could possibly ever deliver. You're hoping she (or he) will provide a completeness that you don't find in God. With such impossible expectations marriage is bound to bring disappointment. "My lover is mine, and I am his," says the young woman in Song of Songs 2:16; 6:3 (NLT). It is a lovely thing to be able to say. But there is a much better thing to be able to say: "I still belong to [God]," and "he is mine forever" (Psalm 73:23, 26 NLT).

Is God enough for you in your marriage? Maybe you're married and have found marriage to be a disappointment. It may well be that there's nothing much wrong with your spouse except that you were investing too much in her. God wasn't enough for you and so you looked for fulfillment, pleasure and satisfaction in marriage. But your spouse is not God and never can be. And so you've turned to porn to deliver what your marriage couldn't. But the real question is: is God enough for you?

Get a big vision. Human beings were made in God's image to reflect God's glory. But humanity rejected God.

> For although they knew God, they neither glorified him as God nor gave thanks to him, but their thinking became futile and their foolish hearts were darkened. Although they claimed to be wise, they became fools and exchanged the glory of the immortal God for images made to look like mortal man and birds and animals and reptiles.
>
> Therefore God gave them over in the sinful desires of their hearts to sexual impurity for the degrading of their bodies with one another. (Romans 1:21-24)

We chose not to glorify God but to seek our own pitiful glory instead. We exchanged the glory of the immortal God and looked instead for glory in created things. This wrecked our relationship with God—we became his enemies. And it wrecked our sex lives. Sex has become for us a pursuit of vainglory, with devastating results. When we reject God's glory our sex lives go awry.

By God's grace we are not left in this miserable state. Christ entered our world as the true image of God, to remake us in God's image. "If anyone is in Christ," says Paul, "he is a new creation; the old has gone, the new has come!" (2 Corinthians 5:17). We were created in God's image, but we've made a mess of being in God's image, and as a result we've made a mess of our sexuality. But in Christ there is a new creation. We're being re-created in God's image to again reflect God's glory. Mark Driscoll encourages us to put one end of a stick into a fire:

> When that end gets hot and glowing red from glorying in the fire until its heat and light are transferred to it, take it out and look at it. Remind yourself that when the Bible says you are the glory of God, it means that you are like that stick and supposed to draw near to the pure and powerful God who is your Father and radiate his heat and light to the world.
>
> You are not an animal. You are the glory of God.
> You are not a pervert. You are the glory of God.
> You are not an addict. You are the glory of God.
> You are not a victim. You are the glory of God.
> You are not a fool. You are the glory of God.[12]

Don't just try to stop using porn, important though that is. Let me suggest that you get a vision for something much bigger: a vision of reflecting Christ's glory in the world. Only this will be big enough to eclipse the appeals of porn.

What happens if you weigh a life with porn against a life without porn? Put like that, porn will always win, for it offers excitement, pleasure, thrills. A life without porn is a life without those excitements, pleasures and thrills; by definition a "without" life, a lesser life.

But a life without porn is not the true alternative to a life with porn. We should instead be weighing a life with porn against a life lived for God's glory. Porn versus glory, porn versus God, fleeting pleasure versus lasting pleasure, shame versus glory, destruction versus eternal life: which looks the lesser life now? "I reoriented myself to who God is," says Ed, "and what he's done for a sinful world. This has been very successful in reducing my need for porn and also giving real purpose to my emptiness—to exist for the glory of God alone."

Why is the universe so big? A light year is the distance traveled by light in one year. This works out at 5.879 trillion miles. The distance between New York and London is 3,468 miles. So to travel the equivalent of a light year you would have to travel from New York to London 1,695 *million* times. Our galaxy is approximately 100,000 light years across. The next galaxy beyond our own is two million light years away. And there are thought to be at least 100,000 million galaxies in the universe.

Why is the universe so big? Is it all really necessary? There seems such a redundancy of space.

The answer, according to Psalm 19:1, is that "the heavens declare the glory of God; the skies proclaim the work of his hands." Solomon says, "The heavens, even the highest heaven, cannot contain you" (1 Kings 8:27). The scale of the universe is beyond anything we can get our heads around. Yet Solomon says it's not big enough to contain God. Isaiah says God has measured the universe by his handbreadths (Isaiah 40:12).

It's not only the vast scale of the universe that declares the glory of God. Consider a single leaf. Look at it closely. Look at the way the veins trace across under its surface. Amazing. Each leaf is unique, a thing of beauty. Now look at a whole forest: hundreds of trees, each with thousands of leaves. Each of those millions of leaves is a thing of exquisite beauty, yet only rarely do we stop to appreciate even one of them. There is in our world a staggering superfluity of beauty, a redundancy of beauty far beyond anything we humans can take in, beauty that serves no purpose except to contribute to God's own pleasure. Consider an individual snowflake. Each one is unique, precision crafted. And then scale that up to a snowy landscape: an extravagant, reckless redundancy of beauty, all for God's glory.

The universe is so big and detailed so that we can glimpse something of its Creator's glory. More than that, it is as it is because God was creating a stage fit for the cross. The Bible says Jesus was slain before the foundation of the world. The cross came first in the plan of God; it was the starting point. To display his grace, God sent his Son to redeem his rebellious people for his eternal glory. Paul's repeated refrain as he lays out the eternal plan of salvation is that it's all "to the praise of [his] glorious grace" (Ephesians 1:6, 12, 14). God's blessing on us, his eternal choice to save us, our adoption into his family, our redemption from sin through the blood of Christ, the forgiveness of sin, the revelation of God's plan, the illumination of our hearts by the Spirit, the new spiritual life that God gives his children, the gift of the Spirit, the hope of a glorious inheritance—all have as their ultimate goal the praise of God's glory. God has seated us with Christ, Paul says, "in order that in the coming ages he might show the incomparable riches of his grace, expressed in his kindness to us in Christ Jesus" (Ephesians 2:7). Creation, history, everything is built for the cross. It's here that God ultimately and most completely displays his glory. Here at the cross we see not only the glory of his power but also the glory of his love. And what stage is appropriate for this central act in the drama of history and eternity? Only a universe of unimaginable scale and detail and beauty.

The universe had to be this big. And what God created millions of stars to do, he also made you to do—to declare his glory. You declare God's glory when you trust his promises, delight in his Word, serve his people, sing his praises, care for his world, proclaim his gospel, call him Father and cry to him for mercy.

And that choice is before you when you're tempted to look at porn. Are you going to choose the shame of porn or the glory of God?

Conclusion

Putting It All Together

WE'VE BEEN LOOKING AT THE KEY ingredients in our battle against pornography (see table 7). Parts four and five are where many people begin, but in fact they're only reinforcements of parts one to three. Yet if they're not there, you're unlikely to sustain change. In fact, it's unlikely that you're serious about stopping porn (part one) if you're not willing to put parts four and five in place. The chances are that no one of these parts will do the job on its own. But together they offer real hope for change.

Look at these stories. All testify to the importance of a multi-faceted strategy with a focus on the affections of our heart.

Table 7. Ingredients in the Battle Against Porn

1	abhorence of porn	a hatred of porn itself (not just the shame it brings) and a longing for change
2	adoration of God	a desire for God, arising from a confidence that he offers more than porn
3	assurance of grace	an assurance that you are loved by God and right with God through faith in the work of Jesus
4	avoidance of temptation	a commitment to do all in your power to avoid temptation, starting with controls on your computer
5	accountability to others	a community of Christians who are holding you accountable and supporting you in your struggle

Sheer willpower didn't work very well. Reminding myself it's a sin also didn't work very well. Ultimately, the thing that helped is when I formed meaningful relationships with other Christians who also had the same struggles with porn and who would be frank about it. Understanding God is in the process of helping me overcome porn was a *big* help. Finally, as I prepared for marriage and came to understand God's design for marriage—about how a man is to love his wife as Jesus loved the church—the whole idea of porn just broke—still breaks—my heart and I wouldn't use it any more.

Talking with other men and having accountability groups help. I have x3watch [accountability software], which keeps me accountable (or forces me to be more sneaky). I also go to Christian counselling, which has helped tremendously. Praying through the real root issues (such as lust or emotional dependency) rather than tackling their manifestations (pornography and masturbation) is probably the only effective method of dealing with it.

I found that working on building a Christian understanding of marriage and sex has helped. Also an understanding of how the sex industry destroys lives. These things have significantly lessened the attraction of porn. It's not what I want any more. The other thing is a closer relationship to God, based on his grace alone transforming me and making me more like his Son. Developing self-control generally. And understanding what triggers temptation and what scenarios to avoid. If I'm tired and bored, I read a good book or watch some sport or a good movie. I have these options planned in advance.

My early efforts consisted in struggling to build up the willpower to resist which, of course, failed miserably. My roommates and I all keeping our computers downstairs in the common room has been effective. This openness helps. But external means can always be circumvented. Meditation on the worth of

Christ and the promises of freedom in the gospel have been the only things I've found to be consistently, deeply effective.

REFLECTION QUESTIONS

1. What effects has porn had in your life? How has it affected your relationship with your spouse? Your family? Other people? How has it affected your relationship with God and his people? (See chap. 1.)

2. What situations trigger your temptation to use porn? How do you justify or excuse your use of porn? What truths counter these excuses? (See chap. 2.)

3. What does porn offer you? How does God offer more? To what truths will you turn in moments of temptation? (See chap. 2.)

4. How do you think God views you? How are you drawing near to your heavenly Father for help? What are you doing to renew your delight in Jesus? How do you experience the leading and enabling of the Holy Spirit? (See chap. 3.)

5. What strategies for avoiding temptation are you putting in place? Are there other areas of your life where you need to develop self-control in addition to the area of porn? What steps are you taking to make better use of the "weapons" of faith in the battle against porn? (See chap. 4.)

6. What measures are you putting in place to ensure that you are accountable and supported in your struggle? Who are you talking to about your struggle with porn? Do you meet regularly? (See chap. 4.)

7. In what ways is God calling you to renew your commitment to live for his glory? How could you better serve your spouse? Your family? Your church? Your neighborhood? (See chap. 5.)

A PRAYER OF CONFESSION

It's time to confess your sin before God and turn back to him in repentance. Take David's prayer of repentance in Psalm 51, after his sexual sin, and make it your own.

Have mercy on me, O God,
   according to your unfailing love;
according to your great compassion
   blot out my transgressions.

How do you view God? How do you think God views you? Meditate on his great compassion. Contrast your failed love for him with his unfailing love to you.

Wash away all my iniquity
   and cleanse me from my sin.
For I know my transgressions,
   and my sin is always before me.

Confess the specifics of your sin. Tell God what you've done and when. Include not only viewing porn, but sexual fantasies, failed responsibilities and any mistreatment of your family.

Against you, you only, have I sinned
   and done what is evil in your sight.

Identify how you've sinned against your spouse, your family, women (or men) in general and your church. Now identify the underlying sin against God. In what ways have you thought porn offered more than God?

so that you are proved right when you speak
   and justified when you judge.

If God were to judge you for your sexual sin, are you persuaded that he would be right to do so? Could you celebrate the justice of his judgment?

Surely I was sinful at birth,
   sinful from the time my mother conceived me.
Surely you desire truth in the inner parts;
   you teach me wisdom in the inmost place.

What have you blamed for your use of porn? What's the ultimate cause? What truths have you failed to believe?

> Cleanse me with hyssop, and I shall be clean;
> wash me, and I will be whiter than snow.

Sin not only makes us guilty, it also makes us unclean. But grace washes us whiter than snow. Who are you? What defines you? What gives you your identity? Does porn shape your identity or Christ?

> Let me hear joy and gladness;
> let the bones you have crushed rejoice.
> Hide your face from my sins
> and blot out all my iniquity.

Listen hard for joy and gladness. From where do they come? What truths counter the false promises of porn in your life? Rehearse those truths until they bring joy and gladness to your heart.

> Create in me a pure heart, O God,
> and renew a steadfast spirit within me.
> Do not cast me from your presence
> or take your Holy Spirit from me.
> Restore to me the joy of your salvation
> and grant me a willing spirit, to sustain me.

Ask God to give you the resources to battle porn. Ask him to give you a sexually pure heart and a steadfast resolve to resist sexual temptation. Ask him to fill you with the presence of his Spirit. Ask him to give the joy in Christ that makes you willing to sustain the fight against sin. Pray especially for those times when you know you're vulnerable to temptation.

> Then I will teach transgressors your ways,
> and sinners will turn back to you.

To whom could you tell your story of salvation? Who could you help? With whom could you be accountable?

> Save me from bloodguilt, O God,

the God who saves me,
and my tongue will sing of your righteousness.
O Lord, open my lips,
and my mouth will declare your praise.

It's time to turn from the self-preoccupation of porn and start celebrating the God who saves. Take time to sing his righteousness and declare his praise.

You do not delight in sacrifice, or I would bring it;
you do not take pleasure in burnt offerings.
The sacrifices of God are a broken spirit;
a broken and contrite heart,
O God, you will not despise.

Have you been trying to earn God's approval? Have you hesitated to come before God after using porn? Come before him now, offering your broken heart. He'll not despise or reject you.

In your good pleasure make Zion prosper;
build up the walls of Jerusalem.
Then there will be righteous sacrifices,
whole burnt offerings to delight you;
then bulls will be offered on your altar.

What could you do to serve in your church? What could you do to serve in your neighborhood? What could you do to build Christ's kingdom? It's time to turn from the self-preoccupation of porn. Close the window on porn and start serving the people of God.

Notes

Introduction: Let's Talk About Porn

[1]Jill C. Manning, "The Impact of Pornography on Women: Social Science Findings and Clinical Observations," pp. 6-7, *A Consultation on the Social Costs of Pornography*, Witherspoon Institute, December 2008 <www.winst.org>.

[2]Norman Doidge, "Acquiring Tastes and Loves: What Neuroplasticity Teaches Us About Sexual Attraction and Love," *A Consultation on the Social Costs of Pornography*, Witherspoon Institute, December 2008, p. 10 <www.winst.org>.

[3]Pamela Paul, *Pornified: How Pornography Is Damaging Our Lives, Our Relationships, and Our Families* (New York: Holt Paperbacks, 2006); Pamela Paul, "From Pornography to Porno to Porn: How Porn Became the Norm," *A Consultation on the Social Costs of Pornography*, Witherspoon Institute, December 2008, p. 2 <www.winst .org>.

[4]Alvin Cooper, "Sexually Compulsive Behaviour," *Contemporary Sexuality* 32, no.4 (1998): 1-3.

[5]"ChristiaNet Poll Finds That Evangelicals Are Addicted to Porn," *Marketwire*, August 7, 2006 <www.marketwire.com/press-release/Christianet-Inc-703951.html>.

[6]Timothy C. Morgan, "Porn's Stranglehold," *Christianity Today*, March 2008.

[7]"Pastors Viewing Internet Pornography," *Leadership Journal* 89 (2001); see also *Christianity Today*, March 5, 2001.

[8]Statistic from XXXchurch.com.

[9]Martin Luther, cited in Michael W. Goheen, "Making Our Own Confession," *Reformed Worship* 77 (2005): 32.

[10]R. Albert Mohler, "The Seduction of Pornography and the Integrity of Christian Marriage," p. 1, March 13, 2004 <www.sbts.edu/documents/Mohler/EyeCovenant .pdf>.

[11]See Tony Payne and Phillip D. Jensen, *Pure Sex* (Sydney, Australia: Matthias Media, 1998), pp. 18-19.

[12]Statistics from XXXchurch.com.

[13]Martin Luther, "True Contemplation of the Cross," *Jesus, Keep Me Near the Cross: Experiencing the Passion and Power of Easter*, ed. Nancy Guthrie (Wheaton, Ill.: Crossway, 2009), pp. 11-12.

Chapter 1: Looking Beyond the Frame

[1]Andrew Comiskey, "From the Famine of Sexual Addiction to the Feast of Life," *Desert Stream* <www.desertstream.org/Publisher/File.aspx?ID=1000011294>.

[2]Steve Gallagher, *At the Altar of Sexual Idolatry* (Dry Ridge, Ky.: Pure Life Ministries, 2007), p. 37.

[3]Craig Gross, *The Dirty Little Secret* (Grand Rapids: Zondervan, 2006), p. 41.

[4]Pamela Paul, "From Pornography to Porno to Porn: How Porn Became the Norm," *A Consultation on the Social Costs of Pornography*, Witherspoon Institute, December 2008, p. 3 <www.winst.org>.

[5]Ibid.

[6]Jill C. Manning, "The Impact of Pornography on Women: Social Science Findings and Clinical Observations," *A Consultation on the Social Costs of Pornography*, Witherspoon Institute, December 2008, p. 11 <www.winst.org>.

[7]Paul, "From Pornography to Porno to Porn," p. 3.

[8]American Psychological Association study, cited in Tim Challies, "A Pornified Culture," *Challies.com*, February 23, 2007 <www.challies.com/archives/articles/two -related-new.php>.

[9]Ana J. Bridges, "Pornography's Effects on Interpersonal Relationships," *A Consultation on the Social Costs of Pornography*, The Witherspoon Institute, December 2008, pp. 3-4 <www.winst.org>.

[10]Robert Jensen, *Getting Off: Pornography and the End of Masculinity* (Cambridge, Mass.: South End Press, 2007), pp. 47-48.

[11]Bridges, "Pornography's Effects on Interpersonal Relationships," pp. 10-11.

[12]Ibid., p. 8.

[13]Manning, "Impact of Pornography on Women," p. 3.

[14]Naomi Wolf, "The Porn Myth," *New York Magazine*, October 20, 2003.

[15]American Psychological Association report, cited in Challies, "A Pornified Culture."

[16]James Wolcott, "Debbie Does Barnes & Noble," *Vanity Fair*, September 2005, p. 127.

[17]See, for example, ibid., pp. 124-27; and Gross, *Dirty Little Secret*.

[18]Gross, *Dirty Little Secret*, p. 77.

[19]Finlo Rohrer, "The Men Who Sleep with Prostitutes," *BBC News Magazine*, February 22, 2008 <http://news.bbc.co.uk/2/hi/7257623.stm>.

[20]Manning, "Impact of Pornography on Women," p. 3.

[21]Martin Saunders, "Gagged and Bound," *Christianity*, February 2009, p. 24. Stop the Traffik is an international campaign against people-trafficking; see www.stopthe traffik.org.

[22]Manning, "Impact of Pornography on Women," pp. 16-17.

[23]Bridges, "Pornography's Effects on Interpersonal Relationships," pp. 15-17.

[24]R. Albert Mohler, "The Seduction of Pornography and the Integrity of Christian Marriage," p. 11, March 13, 2004 <www.sbts.edu/documents/Mohler/EyeCovenant .pdf>.

[25]Wolf, "Porn Myth."

[26]Manning, "Impact of Pornography on Women," p. 16.

[27]Bridges, "Pornography's Effects on Interpersonal Relationships," pp. 15-17.

[28]Paul, "From Pornography to Porno to Porn," p. 3.

[29]Jensen, *Getting Off*, p. 111.

[30]Gross, *Dirty Little Secret*, p. 90.

[31]Ibid., p. 67.

[32]Richard Winter, "The Struggle for Sexual Purity: Pornography," European Leadership Forum, 2005 <www.euroleadershipresources.org/resource.php?ID=288>.

Chapter 2: Freed by the Beauty of God

[1]Mark R. Laaser and Louis J. Gregoire, "Pastors and Cybersex Addiction," *Sexual and Relationship Therapy* 18, no. 3 (2003): 401.

[2]See Tim Chester, *You Can Change: God's Transforming Power for Our Sinful Behaviour and Negative Emotions* (Wheaton, Ill.: Crossway, 2010), chaps. 4-6.

[3]John Piper, *Future Grace* (Colorado Springs: Multnomah, 1995), pp. 334-35.

[4]Augustine, cited in "Pornography and the Quest for Intimacy," *StillDeeper*, March 26, 2008 <www.stilldeeper.com/ja/index.php?option=com_content&view=article &id=24:pornography-a-the-quest-for-intimacy&catid=5:look&Itemid=11>.

[5]G. K. Chesterton, cited by Les Parrott, *Crazy Good Sex* (Grand Rapids: Zondervan, 2009), p. 44.

[6]David White, "Living in the Light: A Redemptive Response to Sexual Sin," *Harvest USA*, 2006, p. 2 <www.harvestusa.org/index.php?option=com_content&view=arti cle&id=129%3Aliving-in-the-light-a-redemptive-response-to-sexual-sin&catid=23%3Apornography-a-sexual-addiction&Itemid=89&limitstart=1>.

[7]David Powlison, *Breaking Pornography Addiction* (Greensboro, N.C.: New Growth Press, 2008).

[8]Craig Lockwood, *Falling Forward: The Pursuit of Sexual Purity* (Grandview, Mo.: Desert Stream Press, 2000), p. 13.

[9]Robert Jensen, *Getting Off: Pornography and the End of Masculinity* (Cambridge, Mass.: South End Press, 2007).

[10]"Pornography and the Quest for Intimacy," *StillDeeper*.

[11]Ibid.

[12]Jensen, *Getting Off*, p. 115.

[13]Gordon MacDonald, *When Men Think Private Thoughts* (Nashville: Thomas Nelson, 1996), pp. 3-9.

[14]Mark Laaser, cited in John W. Kennedy, "Help for the Sexually Desperate," *Christianity Today*, March 7, 2008 <www.christianitytoday.com/ct/2008/march/18.28.html>.

[15]C. S. Lewis, *The Problem of Pain* (New York: Macmillan, 1962), p. 145.

[16]Mark Laaser, cited in Kennedy, "Help for the Sexually Desperate."

[17]Powlison, *Breaking Pornography Addiction.*

[18]Rob Bell, *Sex God: Exploring the Endless Connections Between Sexuality and Spirituality* (Grand Rapids: Zondervan, 2007), p. 78.

[19]Carl Trueman, "No Text Please, I'm British!" *Reformation21,* February 2009 <www.reformation21.org/counterpoints/wages-of-spin/no-text-please-im-british.php>.

[20]"Pornography and the Quest for Intimacy," *StillDeeper.*

[21]Piper, *Future Grace,* p. 336.

Chapter 3: Freed by the Grace of God

[1]John Piper, "Gutsy Guilt," *Christianity Today,* October 19, 2007 <www.christianitytoday.com/ct/2007/october/38.72.html>.

[2]Gordon Cheng, "Sexual Immorality: Some Thoughts from Corinth," *The Briefing* 368 (2009): 13.

[3]This section is adapted from Tim Chester, *You Can Change: God's Transforming Power for Our Sinful Behavior and Negative Emotions* (Wheaton, Ill.: Crossway, 2010), pp. 41-42.

Chapter 4: The Fight of Faith

[1]From Tim Chester, *You Can Change: God's Transforming Power for Our Sinful Behavior and Negative Emotions* (Wheaton, Ill.: Crossway, 2010), pp. 117-18.

[2]Martin Luther, *Lectures on Romans,* Library of Christian Classics 15 (Louisville: Westminster, 1961), p. 128.

[3]John Calvin *Institutes* 3.3.9.

[4]Mark R. Laaser and Louis J. Gregoire, "Pastors and Cybersex Addiction," *Sexual and Relationship Therapy* 18, no. 3 (2003): 401.

[5]Steve Gallagher, *At the Altar of Sexual Idolatry* (Dry Ridge, Ky.: Pure Life Ministries, 2007), p. 37.

[6]David Powlison, *Breaking Pornography Addiction* (Greensboro, N.C.: New Growth Press, 2008).

[7]Rob Bell, *Sex God: Exploring the Endless Connections Between Sexuality and Spirituality* (Grand Rapids: Zondervan, 2007), pp. 81-84.

[8]David White, "Living in the Light: A Redemptive Response to Sexual Sin," *Harvest USA,* 2006, p. 2 <www.harvestusa.org/index.php?option=com_content&view=article&id=129%3Aliving-in-the-light-a-redemptive-response-to-sexual-sin&catid=23%3Apornography-a-sexual-addiction&Itemid=89&limitstart=1>.

[9]Gallagher, *At the Altar of Sexual Idolatry,* pp. 75-76.

[10]White, "Living in the Light."

[11]Dietrich Bonhoeffer, *Life Together, Prayerbook of the Bible,* Works 5 (Minneapolis: Fortress, 2005), p. 108.

[12]Jonathan Dobson, *Fight Clubs: Gospel-Centered Discipleship* (ebook: The Resurgence, 2009), p. 44 <www.theresurgence.com/fightclubs>.

[13]Adapted from Lyndon Bowring, et al., *Living Free* (London: CARE, 2008), p. 51.

Chapter 5: Freed for the Glory of God
[1]Antoine de Saint-Exupéry, cited in David Powlison, *Breaking Pornography Addiction* (Greensboro, N.C.: New Growth Press, 2008).
[2]Julian Hardyman, *Idols* (Nottingham, U.K.: Inter-Varsity Press, 2010).
[3]See Joan Jacobs Brumberg, *The Body Project: An Intimate History of American Girls* (New York: Random House, 1997); and Naomi Wolf, *The Beauty Myth: How Images of Beauty Are Used Against Women* (New York: William Morrow, 1991), pp. 16-17.
[4]Mark Driscoll, "Porn-Again Christian," *Re:Lit*, 2009, p. 5 <http://relit.org/porn_again_christian/downloads/relit_ebook_pac.pdf>.
[5]See Hardyman, *Idols*.
[6]C. S. Lewis, *The Screwtape Letters* (New York: Macmillan, 1944), p. 112.
[7]Ben Patterson, "The Goodness of Sex and the Glory of God," in *Sex and the Supremacy of Christ*, ed. John Piper and Justin Taylor (Wheaton, Ill.: Crossway, 2005), p. 55.
[8]Les Parrott, *Crazy Good Sex* (Grand Rapids: Zondervan, 2009), pp. 73-79.
[9]University of Chicago study, cited in ibid., p. 78.
[10]John Piper, "Single in Christ: A Name Better Than Sons and Daughters," *Desiring God*, April 29, 2007 <www.desiringgod.org/ResourceLibrary/Sermons/ByDate/2007/2162_Single_in_Christ_A_Name_Better_Than_Sons_and_Daughters>.
[11]Adapted from Carolyn McCulley, *Did I Kiss Marriage Goodbye? Trusting God for a Hope Deferred* (Wheaton, Ill.: Crossway, 2004), p. 21.
[12]Driscoll, "Porn-Again Christian," pp. 27-28.